LEFTOVER
Foods:

With Optional and Substitutable Ingredients

Eat Your Way Every Day!

"Everyone wins in this book"

Vanesa V. Melendres

Suite 300 - 990 Fort St
Victoria, BC, Canada, V8V 3K2
www.friesenpress.com

Copyright © 2015 by Vanesa Velacse Melendres
First Edition — 2015

All rights reserved.

No part of this publication may be reproduced in any form, or by any means, electronic or mechanical, including photocopying, recording, or any information browsing, storage, or retrieval system, without permission in writing from the publisher.

ISBN
978-1-4602-6001-2 (Hardcover)
978-1-4602-6002-9 (Paperback)
978-1-4602-6003-6 (eBook)

1. Cooking

Distributed to the trade by The Ingram Book Company

Table of Contents

ACKNOWLEDGEMENT....................**XIV**

INTRODUCTION......................**XVII**

**USEFUL TIPS AND INFORMATION
ABOUT CULTURES, FAITHS AND FOOD RULES** **1**

GUIDELINES AND ILLUSTRATIONS **25**
    BREAKFAST.........................28
    BRUNCH...........................29
    LUNCH 30
    DINNER............................31
    PACK LUNCH OR PACK MEALS 32
    YOGURT STORAGE 36
    EGGS..............................36

PAN DE SAL BREAD DOUGH
(OPTIONAL AND SUBSTITUTABLE INGREDIENTS)
..................................38

HOW TO MAKE CASSAVA RICE
(SWEET POTATO RICE AND TARO RICE)
(OPTIONAL AND SUBSTITUTABLE INGREDIENTS)
..................................40

CAULIFLOWER RICE....................41

HOW TO MAKE LIQUID STOCKS
(OPTIONAL AND SUBSTITUTABLE INGREDIENTS)
..................................43

HOW TO MAKE ALMOND FLOUR............44

HOW TO MAKE BREADS DOUGH
FOR PALEO DIET, GLUTEN FREE DIET, DIABETIC,
MACROBIOTIC DIET, VEGETARIAN, HALAL OR
KOSHER..............................45

TWO WAY OF COOKING THE CASSAVA RICE
(WITH LIQUIDS OR WITHOUT LIQUID).......47

FOOD PREPARATION TIME GUIDE 49

LEFTOVER FOOD RECIPES 51

    FRESH ROLLED SALAD WITH FRESH AVOCADO .53

    HOT CARROT SOUP WITH CABBAGE.........55

    GUACAMOLE............................57

    GUACAMOLE APPETIZER..................59

    HOW TO SAVE LEFTOVER FRESH AVOCADO....61

    ONION GRAVY WITH CRACKERS...........63

COLOR CODED BELL PEPPER 65

NASI LEMAK MODERN STYLE
(MALAYSIAN COCONUT RICE) 67

DRY VEGETABLE ADOBO 71

BRUNCH LEFTOVER BREAD 73

STIR-FRIED SPAGHETTI 75

FRIED RICE WITH VEGETABLES 77

CHOCOLATE FONDUE 79

BRUNCH BAKED SUSHI MINI CUPCAKES 81

CHUNKY CREAMY SWEET POTATOES 83

HOT RICE ARROZ CALDO (PORRIDGE) 85

POTATOES WITH SOUR CREAM 87

FEAST WRAP 89

EGG SANDWICH 91

MEXICAN WRAPPED TACO 93

FRUIT COCKTAIL QUESADILLAS 95

CHEESE FONDUE WITH LEFTOVER BREAD 97

VEGETABLE SOUP WITH MACARONI 99

WRAPPED LEFTOVER FOODS 101

BAKED SALMON 103

FRENCH ONION SOUP 105

PAN DE SAL BREADS 107

PAN DE SAL DE MEXICO FAJITAS 109

PAN DE SAL DE PILIPINAS ADOBO 111

PAN DE SAL DE QUESO (CHEESE BREAD) 113

PAN DE SAL BAVARIA GERMANY 115

PAN DE SAL DE VEGETARIAN 117

DUMMIES KITCHEN DIARIES **118**

12 When they had plenty to eat, Jesus said to his disciples, "Gather up the leftover pieces, so that nothing will be wasted." **13** So they gathered them and filled twelve baskets with the pieces of the five barley loaves that had been left over by those who had eaten. **14** When the people saw that he had done a miraculous sign, they said, "This is truly the prophet who is coming into the world." **John 6:12-14.**

Thank you for purchasing "Leftover foods" with optional and substitutable ingredients. Eat your way everyday and everyone wins in this book.

<u>I am proud to share this book with everyone. I have done extensive research and gained a lot of insight doing my own experiments. I applied my experience and I am sharing and educating the readers so that they have a better understanding of what they are eating.</u>

<u>We are living in a fast paced, fast food environment and I am proposing a healthier way of eating using "leftover foods".</u>

Matthew 25:35-40 New King James Version (NKJV)

"**35** for I was hungry and you gave Me food; I was thirsty and you gave Me drink; I was a stranger and you took Me in; **36** I *was* naked and you clothed Me; I was sick and you visited Me; I was in prison and you came to Me.'

37 "Then the righteous will answer Him, saying, 'Lord, when did we see you hungry and feed *you*, or thirsty and give *you* drink? **38** When did we see you a stranger and take *you* in, or naked and clothe *you*? **39** Or when did we see you sick, or in prison, and come to you?' **40** And the King will answer and say to them, 'Assuredly, I say to you, inasmuch as you did *it* to one of the least of these my brethren, you did *it* to me.'"

LEFTOVER
Foods:

With Optional and Substitutable Ingredients

**My family and friends who taught me in all
the way are always be in my heart**

Especially my three lovely children Max, Sophia and Marcus

My inspiration forever.

Acknowledgement

First I want to thank GOD for all the guidance by answering all my prayers in the writing of this book so I can share with everybody around the world in this sensible way of living on this planet to know the REALITIES and LOGICAL WAYS that we should be wary to make senses in these aspects.

All my blessings to all the FriesenPress team who taught me how to put it all together, since this was my first experience ever in writing a book, and educating me with their knowledge and experience by channeling my thoughts and ideas and transposing them on paper. Especially the people who worked with me since the first day and to all their staff who were all involved in the development of this incredible book from a simple idea. I was very impressed by all the involvement of each other to work as a team. Thank you so much!

My deepest gratitude to the Alberta Children's Hospital Foundation Canada and the whole staff of the Alberta Children's Hospital here in Calgary who were always there to give help and support the needs for the bedridden children, and especially by taking care of my daughter Sophia Anne Beatty for her disability and giving her hope that she will walk sooner and big help with covering a large portion of the very costly major surgery procedures. Through this generosity from Alberta Children's Hospital Foundation, I voluntarily pledge to donate back to the foundation who provided help for my daughter that each book sold, I will give away a portion of my proceeds to help more kids in need thus keep supporting the Alberta Children's Hospital Foundation in their mission.

My gratitude goes to my homeland Philippines Samar Island where I was raised. The same region where I was born that was badly slammed by the Super typhoon Yolanda (Haiyan international name). All my thoughts are in helping them as well, especially children needing better education. I will resume the education fundraisers initiated by my father (Arthur Bodoy Moralde Melendres) before his unfortunate departure. I will make him proud in carrying on the aid he organized for the scholarship program, children's care and support.

My grateful thanks to all my classmates who worked as a group in sharing ideas especially my Home Economics teacher, Mrs. Marcia Joriza for all her contribution and knowledge to all her students 1997-2000 and to the Malaga National High School Calbayog City, Western Samar Philippines Culinary Arts Course department. Thank you so much to my entire teaching staff back in my high school days.

My deepest heartfelt love and thanks to my family back in the Philippines for their real love and support like my mother Alma Velacsi Melendres and my siblings. My blessed grace to my three lovely children, Special thanks to their father Mr. Layton Wayne Beatty by supporting me in this project of mine and very thankful to all his family here in Calgary, Canada especially to his siblings and parents Mr. and Mrs. Arthur and Mertie Beatty for all their help by referring and introducing me to FriesenPress Publishing Company who arranged my book in a professional manner.

I wish all my grateful words and respects to everyone. I am fully pleased with happiness that this book is finally completed. If by writing more books of this type, I can improve more people's lives, I will continue to do so. In this manner these people are winners. THAT IS MY MISSION.

Introduction

Although we see a lot of cookbooks on retail bookstore shelves or online with different and unique ways of cooking, no one has written about dealing with "leftover foods", including optional and substitutable ingredients. It is not just about saving food from being thrown out or to save money, it is also about creating tasty and healthy fast food using the leftover food in your cupboards, fridge or freezer.

My *aim* and *goal* in writing this book is to help everyone recognize that the ingredients you have in your kitchen can be "Optional and Substitutable Ingredients" in many of the recipes in this book.

Optional ingredients are those you can use if you have them on hand. *Substitutable* ingredients are those you are allowed to eat according to your dietary practices (e.g. vegan, gluten free, kosher).

When I think about leftover foods this way I want people to realize that you can eat in a way that respects your health, diet and faith-based dietary rules. It is about choosing ingredients and adding them to a recipe that makes sense for your health or lifestyle.

A note of caution: More and more we are being educated to become aware of what food we should eat through television and the Internet. Some information is false or misleading so you have to be careful what you believe and adopt.

People have asked why I think this way...

In our multicultural society, food plays a special role across any number of faiths and dietary practices. I want to help people and leave no one behind in being able to use leftover foods in a way that respects their beliefs and practices.

Who are they that they cannot eat whatever we serve at our table?

- Faith-based dietary practices
- Muslims and halal food
- Jewish people and Kosher food
- Paleo diet
- Macrobiotic diet
- Diabetic diet
- Vegetarians and a vegetarian diet
- People with Celiac disease and a gluten free diet
- People with gluten intolerance or gluten sensitivity
- Health conscious
- Fitness program diets
- People who are not well
- Children who can't eat what adults can have
- Picky people

Whoever we are in this world we should be aware whether the food we eat is good or healthy for our body. Whatever, whoever we are we all want to have a wonderful and creative meal on our table.

Leftover Foods

I was encouraged to pursue this cookbook project by a member of my church, who reminded me that all religions have something to say about food and especially about the importance of not wasting it. Consider:

> **The Holy Bible:** *When Jesus was feeding the five thousand people, he reminded his disciples: "Gather up the leftover food pieces, so that nothing will be wasted."* John 6:12 (NKJV)

> **The Quran:** *O children of Adam! Look to your adornment at every time and place of worship, and eat and drink but exceed not the bounds: surely, He does not love those who exceed the bounds.* Chapter 7:32 Al-A`RAF

All religions reference the importance of conserving food, including leftovers. It is an important lifestyle choice, particularly when you consider that there are malnourished people all over the world. Religion aside, it is just common sense to open your eyes and realize the reality that millions are suffering every day without enough food to survive. And yet, every day, hundreds of thousands of tons of food go to waste.

Research has shown that a healthy lifestyle includes having decent and nutritious foods at each meal on a daily basis. Our bodies need a steady flow of nutrients to support our immune systems. Skipping meals or snacking on unhealthy food is not good for health.

Having leftover foods ready in your fridge can reduce the temptation to snack on something that is not healthy, like chips or chocolate bars. Taking a few minutes to prepare something using leftover food can help ensure something is ready when the hunger pangs hit.

It is true that we love to eat our traditional foods! All of us have cultural differences and preparing meals – especially traditional foods that we grew up with that take hours to prepare – is often not possible when your time is limited by all the other things you have to do. We all know them: hardworking people, busy full-time mothers, retired people and students living alone and studying full-time. If you are like me, you are one of them!

I hope that this book will help you look at the food in your kitchen in a new way. Think of how to save all your leftover foods, not just the ones after a dinner or party celebration. You'll want to see your intentional leftover food preparation as a way to save time and bring consistency to your daily diet.

This book will guide you and give you tips and healthy information. Some guidelines with illustrations will help you learn about cooking even if you cannot spend an hour in your kitchen. It will help ensure you can put three healthy meals together each day, leaving you more time to focus on other priorities.

Why Leftover Foods?

Food that remains after the rest has been consumed can be saved and used for healthy fast food. This is not the same as fast food from a store or takeout place. It is food that was prepared one way (e.g. barbeque) and now will be prepared a different way to preserve flavor and taste. Other leftover foods include those that have only been partly used and can be combined with other leftover ingredients to make a whole new and tasty dish.

We all need to eat and we all want to save our hard-earned money. And we all enjoy new dishes and flavors. As I started developing this cookbook, I wanted it to be something positive, with helpful ideas and a view that we can all be winners when it comes to making choices about healthy eating and lifestyles. Encouraging people to experiment with these recipes, add optional ingredients or substituting ingredients will help us explore food in a whole new way. It puts the choice in your hands: you choose what is good for your health and substitute as you wish.

So, let us work and learn together!

What Are the Benefits of Leftover Foods?

Time – Leftover foods consume less time because they are pre-cooked so you spend less time in the kitchen getting your food ready.

Leftover Foods

Trends – Food trends have changed over the generations, changing from traditional to fast food. Preparing meals and snacks from leftovers is really the easiest and most creative but still healthy way to eat. Leftover foods can be convenient to our modern lifestyle.

Ideas – I have a lot of new ideas here with sample recipes, pictures and easy to understand instructions so that you can create recipes from your own ideas.

Flavor and taste – Leftover foods are homemade and already have some flavoring like when you BBQ, roast – including meat, fish and vegetables – or grill. It is up to you to determine the techniques to create the food that has the taste you want in your fast leftover foods in a healthy way.

Optional ingredients and substitutable ingredients – You are the one who will decide to add ingredients or substitute ingredients to follow your health needs or faith practices.

Saves money – In general, yes. Especially if the food was originally discounted because it is near its 'best before' date. Half off vegetables make excellent stews and soups at … half the cost!

But the real points to remember are: Reality and Logic. A lot of people around the world do not have enough to eat. We cannot throw out our leftover foods just because we don't know how to prepare them in a new and tasty way. Let us face reality and approach it logically.

For example BBQ or roast. When you first cooked it and there were leftover foods from that way of cooking, would it still the same taste if you BBQ or roast them again? The answer is NO! Not the same and it will become tasteless because it is dried up and the texture and quality is no longer in that food.

How about the nutrition of the food when you cook it the same way again from the first time? It kills all the nutrients of the foods when you do it repeatedly. Better to save by making it a different way by adding certain ingredients depending on what you have on hand and what fits your dietary practices.

Final Words

When I was in high school, we all took a mandatory course in Home Economics. In the Philippines, it's called T.H.E. Fortunately for me and my classmates; we had a very good teacher who took us through all our courses. Beginning in second year in 1997, we learned culinary skills through two-hour lectures three times a week for nine months.

In third year, we worked in groups to prepare various recipes, cook them and present them to the class. Through experiments, observation, reports and demonstration we learned from each other about the dishes we made, with support from our teacher.

Then, in fourth year 1999-2000, our teacher taught us about preservation, delicacies, appetizers, and special techniques and production with substitutable ingredients. It was amazing. She was a very calm and relaxed teacher who ignited in me a lifelong love for cooking and creative cuisine. I still have friends from my home economics classes especially my Home Economics teacher, she is still my friend until now.

This book took a lot of courage for me to write. I want to bring you awareness and help you save time, challenge you to make your own creations and encourage you to share ideas you got from this book.

This book is aimed at helping you to open your mind to create amazing dishes with your leftover foods and give you ideas to create new dishes on your own. I have left a few blank pages in the book at the end so you can write down your own first creative creation recipe from your leftover foods. This book will serve too as a valuable book to pass along to your family as your kitchen diaries.

We have a website too for blogging and sharing photos and ideas you have learned and created from this book. Need some advice? We will help because the key here is to learn from one another and share ideas.

Useful Tips and Information about Cultures, Faiths and Food Rules

Approaching our leftover foods based on the reality around us in the world, and the logical ways we can adapt recipes using optional and substitutable ingredients, applies to everyone: the health conscious, people following a particular fitness program such as CrossFit, eating halal or Kosher, eating gluten free, being vegetarian or supporting the dietary needs of babies, children, seniors and those with medical conditions.

What is Vegetarianism?

People who do not eat some meat and sometimes other animal products, especially for moral, religious or health reasons are called vegetarian. Vegetarians abstain from the consumption of meat including red meat, poultry, seafood and the flesh of any animals. It may also include abstention from by-products of animal slaughter. There are several divisions in the diets of vegetarians:

> ***Ovo vegetarianism*** – includes eggs but not dairy products.
>
> ***Lacto vegetarianism*** – includes dairy products but not eggs.
>
> ***Ovo- lacto vegetarianism or lacto-ovo*** – Includes animal/dairy products such as eggs, milk and honey.
>
> ***Veganism*** – A person who does not eat or use animal products. Such as bone-char refined white sugar or animal-tested baking soda, excludes all animal flesh and products, such as

milk, honey, eggs, as well as items refined or manufactured through any such products.

Jain vegetarianism – A non-theistic religion founded in India in the 6th century BC by Jina Vardhamana Mahariva as a reaction against the teaching of orthodox Brahmanism, and still practiced there.

The Jain religion teaches salvation by perfection through successive lives, and non-injury to living creatures, and is noted for its ascetics. They exclude root vegetables, include dairy but exclude eggs and honey as well.

Raw veganism – fresh and uncooked fruit, seeds, nuts, and vegetables. Vegetables can only be cooked up to a certain temperature.

Fruitarianism – only fruits and other plants matter that can be gathered without harming the plant and permits only fruits, seeds and nuts.

Buddhist vegetarianism – Has no creator god and gives a central role to the doctrine of karma. Many interpret the concept "NOT TO KILL" to require abstinence from meat but not all.

What are Macrobiotic diets?

Consulting, relating to, or following a diet of whole pure prepared foods that is based on Taoist principles of the balance of yin and yang. Involves eating grains and staple food to their dietary regime to be supplemented with vegetables and to avoid animal products, processed foods, refined foods and inorganic.

Macrobiotic diet it is universal principles and standard but they have main food that they believe that it gives more energy or which discover their direction that leads the true happiness for their personal compass to self-discovery like:

Principles of opposites,
Principles of change
Principles of Cycles
Principles of Non-Identity
Principles of front and back

Macrobiotic Diet Main staple principle food likes;

Whole grains to consumed approximately 25-30 percent per volume

Beans Consumed approximately 5 to 10 percent beans either canned or dried

Vegetables consumed approximately 35 percent per day from roots, greens and all varieties of ground vegetables

Macrobiotic Diet Secondary food likes;

Oils 10 percent per day
Nuts 10 percent per day
Seeds 10 percent per day
Fruits 10 percent per day
Beverage like Grain-based by herbal, vegetable juice, Tea

Macrobiotic Diet should strictly avoided

Processed Fruit Juice
Cheese produced by animals
Milk produced by animals
Maple syrup
Agave syrup
Rice syrup
Barley malt
Any refined sugar brown or white
Heavy spices
Medications like pharmautical
Alcohol
Caffeine

Refined oils
Rice
White flour

What is a Gluten Free Diet?

Gluten free is a diet without gluten, a protein composite found in rye, barley, wheat and related grains. Gluten helps wheat to become sticky and is mostly used for making breads, pies, cookies, cakes, rolls, etc. Gluten is also found in a number of food ingredients including mustard, ice cream, Worstershire sauce and even ketchup. It can also be found in non-food items including prescription medicine. If a person is diagnosed with Celiac Disease or Gluten Sensitivity they must eliminate or avoid foods that contain gluten.

Some 1.6 million Americans have decided to start eating gluten free as a means to weight loss or because of gastrointestinal issues. Eating gluten free has never been easier with the market in gluten free products expanding exponentially.

A gluten free diet still includes a wide variety of choice, including:

Meats	Coconuts	Sweet potato rice
Rice	Honey	Coconut flour
Tapioca	Fresh herbs and spices	Taro rice
Corn or cornmeal	Fruits jams and marmalades	Coconut amonis soy sauce
Vegetables and Fruits	Molasses	Tomato puree
Plain nuts and seeds	Dairy products	Maple syrup
Legumes	Pure oils and fats	Tomato paste
Eggs	Sugar	Whole kernel corn
Fish	Almond flour	Yeast fresh and dried
Potatoes	Agave nectar	Gluten free tamari soy sauce
Quinoa	Arrowroot	Gluten free noodles
Buckwheat	Cauliflower rice	Gluten free vinegars
Sorghum	Cassava rice	Stock, cubes, bouillon

Many products are now labeled if they are gluten free. However, some foods may contain hidden gluten, such as:

Cornstarch	Hotdogs, sausages and salami
Hydroxypropyl menthylcellullose	Stocks, cubes and bullions
Baking powder	Ginger ale
Barley flavored candy	Brown rice syrup
Flavored waters	French fries
Cheese spreads	Some potato chips
Beer	Sour cream (especially no fat/low fat)

Are Xanthan gums and Guar gums okay?

Xanthan gum is produced through bacterial fermentation. Xanthomonas camprestries is the bacteria and causes a variety of plant diseases. This is aerobic and is known to cause black rot in crucifers, darkening the vascular tissues of the plants. Xanthan has many important uses in the food industry including making gluten free bread. In some people, however, it causes digestive problems and gas that can be just as bad as their reaction to gluten.

Guar gum comes from the guar bean and is often seen in Indian and Pakistani cuisine.

If your body doesn't tolerate these gums, you can still thicken food dishes using tapioca flour and other natural ingredients.

Tips and Advice

The best thing to do is read the labels to learn the food ingredients and ensure when you eat in public that family, friends and servers are aware that you eat gluten free. Gluten free people should not mix their food with gluten if they are very sensitive. For some, even just a few crumbs of gluten in their foods gives a bad reaction.

You should separate your stock in the pantry and fridge for gluten free, even when you use your kitchenware you should wash properly to degluten especially your household kitchen utensils and tools that are used for cooking ingredients with gluten.

Cooking utensils and tools made of glass or stainless steel are much easier to clean and are 100 percent clean after washing with hot water and soap than cast iron or aluminum pots and pans these can take a year or so to de-gluten because of the materials absorbing it.

What is Celiac Disease?

Celiac disease is a complex genetic autoimmune disease attacking the small intestine due to the presence of gluten. For those medically diagnosed with the condition, gluten must be completely eliminated from the diet and other products including some soaps, toothpaste, shampoos, etc. The symptoms of Celiac disease are primarily gastrointestinal with common symptoms including constipation, migraine headache, fatigue, bloating, diarrhea, infertility and numbness around the mouth.

What is Non-Celiac Gluten Sensitivity?

This is a separate condition from Celiac disease but it is almost the same in removing gluten from the diet and, for some, products touching the skin. The symptoms are mostly in the digestive system, plus skin problems like rashes, heartburn, constipation, stomachache and diarrhea. Some people experience brain fog (like Celiac disease symptoms), gluten depression and anxiety.

What are Halal Foods?

In Islamic law, *halal* means permissible. In the context of food, it means the act of killing, preparing, storing and eating food and there are rules governing each aspect. The foods addressed are mostly types of meats and animal tissue. Foods must be certified by a halal supplier to prove to Muslims they may consume the products without any hesitation. It is a long process because they investigate how the product is made and the source of materials to determine if it's permissible.

The animal must be slaughtered with a sharp knife by cutting the throat, windpipe and the blood vessels in the neck, causing the animal's death without cutting the spinal cord. Lastly the blood from the veins must be drained.

Muslims must also ensure that all foods (particularly processed foods), as well as non-food items like cosmetics and pharmaceuticals are halal. Frequently these products contain animal by-products or other ingredients that are not permissible for Muslims to eat or use on their bodies.

For six years, I lived and worked in Kuala Lumpur, Malaysia. I worked for a French perfume manufacturer that was certified by "JAKIM HALAL" just to follow Islamic procedure.

Non-halal foods:

- Pork
- Blood
- Intoxicants and alcoholic beverages
- Animals killed incorrectly and/or without their God names name being pronounced in their killing.
- Animals slaughtered in the name of anyone but their God's name. All that has been dedicated or offered in sacrifice to an idolatrous altar or saint or a person considered to be "Divine"
- Carrion (carcasses of dead animals, e.g. animals that died in the wild).
- An animal that has been strangled, beaten (to death), killed by a fall, electrocution, gored (to death) or savaged by a beast of prey (unless finished off by a human).
- Ducks
- Meats offered by Christians and Jews

What are Kosher Foods?

Kosher foods conform to the regulations called *Kashrut* (Jewish dietary law). Food that may be consumed according to halakha (Jewish law) is termed *kosher* in English, from the Ashkenazi pronunciation of the Hebrew term *kasher*. Meaning "fit" (for consumption). Food not in accordance with Jewish law is called *treif* (Yiddish: *treyf*, derived from Hebrew *trafah*).[1]

Some of the list of kosher foods is found in the book of Leviticus 11:1-47 and Deuteronomy 14:3-20, as are also certain kosher rules. Food not considered kosher includes the presence of ingredients derived from non-kosher animals or from kosher animals that were not slaughtered in a ritually proper manner; a mixture of meat and milk; wine and grape juice (or their derivatives) produced without supervision; the use of produce from Israel that has not been tithed, or, the use of non-kosher cooking utensils and machinery.[2]

Deuteronomy and Leviticus state that any animal, which chews the cud and has a cloven hoof, is ritually clean, but animals that can only chew the cud or only have cloven hooves are not. Unclean animals include the hare, camel, hyrax, and pig even the camel is a ruminant and has two toes, and the hare and hyrax are hindgut fermenters rather than ruminants.[3]

The Torah lists winged creatures, which may not be consumed, mainly birds of prey, fish-eating water birds, and bats. Leviticus and Deuteronomy state that anything residing in the water, seas and rivers is ritually clean but only if it has both fins and scales.

Leviticus states that every creeping thing that crawls the earth is unclean, however a bug born inside a fruit may be eaten if it has never crawled on the ground. All flying creeping things are considered ritually unclean, according to both Leviticus and Deuteronomy. Leviticus has a list of four exceptions, including locusts.

---

1 Wikipedia: http://en.wikipedia.org/wiki/Kosher_foods.

2 Ibid.

3 Ibid.

Considered Non-Kosher If;

Animal Products

The Talmudic writers banned animal produce as ritually unclean from unhealthy animals. Animals are considered non-kosher if after being slaughtered they are discovered to have disease. Eggs from ritually pure animals would be always prelate.

Dairy Products

If the animal is not slaughtered in the proper way or discovered with disease after being slaughtered, milk will be non-kosher too. If the animal is kosher the milk is kosher too but Orthodox has released a statement declaring the milk permissible based on leniencies.

Human Breast Milk

Human breast milk of any kind is permitted. Breast milk may be consumed directly from the breasts only by children younger than four years old but if the child is sick around five years old it is permitted and older children are only permitted to continue to suckle if they had not stopped doing so for more than three consecutive days.[4]

Cheese

Cheese is a bit complicated. To identify which one is kosher involves rennet, an enzyme which splits milk into curds and whey. If kosher animals are not slaughtered according to the *halakha* the rennet is not kosher. In the conservative practice of Orthodox Jews who observe the *kashrut* laws, they only eat cheese if they are certain the rennet itself was kosher but Isaac Klein's *tshuva* authorized the use of cheese made from non-kosher rennet and this is widely practiced by observant conservative Jews and constitutions.

Rennet is a complex of enzymes produced in a mammalian stomach, which is used in the production of most cheeses.

---

4   Ibid.

Eggs

Eggs are considered *pareve*[5] (neutral) despite being animal products. Mayonnaise is usually *pareve* because it contains eggs.

Gelatin

Gelatin is hydrolyzed collagen. The main protein in animal connective tissue. Today, manufacturers are producing gelatin from the skins of kosher fish.[6]

Blood

In Jewish kosher rules, blood is forbidden to eat on account of the life in the blood. This is banned and the reason is listed twice in Leviticus as well as in Deuteronomy. To wash the blood off the meat is to wash with kosher salt and leave for 20 minutes and shake most off and wash the meat twice to complete the extraction of the blood.

What is Paleo diet?

Following a Paleo diet means eating only natural foods and nothing processed. The diet consists of meats, vegetables, fruits, nuts, fish, and seeds. The diet is healthful as well as not harmful to our bodies. Based on my research, the paleo diet is good for our health and good for the environment and our planet. Removing processed food from your diet also removes a lot of packaging.

The Paleo diet can be adapted for all health and faith practices. It can be gluten free, it can be adapted for diabetics and for everyone who has specific religion-based food practices because you choose your ingredients systematically for making ideal food for your lifestyle.

In my family genetics we have diabetes and cardiovascular disease (CVD). Now in my thirties, I am very careful about what I eat and very conscious

---

[5] **Pareve** - means "neutral", as in prepared without meat, milk, or their derivatives and therefore permissible to be eaten with both meat and dairy dishes according to dietary laws.

[6] Wikipedia. http://en.wikipedia.org/wiki/Kosher_foods.

Leftover Foods

of what I should eat. I watch for how my body reacts to what I eat. During my research for this book, I thought about my loving father who passed away three years ago and my grandfather who passed away just six months later with CVD. It's not easy to have this kind of disease; that's why it's important to continue research and trials to educate us to know about food and diet no matter our religious or cultural beliefs.

From my observation one thing is we depend too much on are processed foods. Nowadays, fast food has taken over the food chain, leaving us unaware of what we are eating or what is in the food we eat. With our fast food diets, we aren't thinking about a healthy way of cooking.

Buying processed food like sauce to use for barbequing makes it easy to burn the meat or vegetables! You know why it's easy to burn and half is cooked and half is uncooked? Because this processed sauce is loaded with sugar. The same with soft drinks or processed powdered juices because they contain a lot of sugar.

Cooking naturally is the best! Avoid processed foods from the supermarket. They are full of sugar and salt. And don't depend on processed spices. I noticed that before and I am sharing here that Yes! I did use many spices from the supermarket shelves before and when I check my pantry at home, WOW! There were tons of difference spices that I can't really use.

If you are Paleo diet you can't consume this following foods:

Grains and Gluten – Because grains contains toxin that become autoimmune and irritation of your digestive system like a person who is diagnose with Celiac disease and Gluten non-sensitivity or intolerant. Mostly it is an inflammatory protein like gluten that they can damage your gut lining and cause of reaction through your skin, or whole body or release insulin that can be triggers fat storage.

Paleo diet; Types of Grains not consumable are;

Barley	Corn
Rice	Rye

Potato	Millet
Quinoa	Oats
Amaranth	Teff
Bulgur	Spelt
Buckwheat	Sorghum
Wheat	Processed food
Legumes	Black beans
Broad beans	Navy beans
Lentils	Lima beans
Garbanzos Beas like Chickpeas)	
Mung beans	Peanut or Peanut butter
Pinto Beans	White beans
Soybeans,	Tofu
Tempeh	Natto
Soy sauce	Miso
Edamame	Soy milk
Agave	Molasses
All Artificial sugars in the boxes or sachet	
Raw sugar	NutraSweet or Equal
Rice syrup	Brown sugar
Sucralose (Splenda)	Corn Syrup
High fructose corn syrup	Sugarcane
Stevia	White sugar
Maple syrup	Maltodextrin
Canola oil	Peanut oil
Corn oil	Soybean oil
Trans fats	Safflower oil
Cottonseed oil	Margarine
Palm kernel oil	Vegetable shortening
Partially hydrogenated oil Sunflower oil	
Whisky	Grain-based vodka
Beer	Gin
Overly slated foods	refined vegetable oils
Candy	Junk foods
Paleo Pantry list:	

Leftover Foods

Cassava flour	Extra-virgin olive oil
Tapioca flour/starch	Broth/stock like Beef, chicken and vegetables
Butter (organic, grass-fed)	Arrowroot
Coconut aminos	canned chiles
Coconut flour	canned sardines
Coconut butter	canned tomatoes
Coconut oil	Avocado oil
Coconut flakes (Unsweetened)	Pickles
Coconut milk	Nuts
Dried fruits	Almond flour
Eggs	Salsa
Spices	Olives
Tomato paste	Nuts
Not processed Meat	Cheese organic or vegetables
Cream cheese	Sour cream
Grass-fed meat	Fresh fruits
Seeds	Flaxseeds oil
Seafood/Fish	Macadamia oil
Golden Flaxseed meal	apple cider vinegar

What is Diabetic Diet?

A person who have problem in the blood sugar and means medical nutrition therapy (MNT), from the meal planning to maintain to moderate the nutritious foods and to watch the carbohydrates intake. Diabetes diet emphasis on whole grains, vegetables, meats and fruits that has low fats, calories and eating rich nutrients. You should be aware to know if the food you are eating is low fat or high fat because if you are diabetic you should consumed the amount of low fat foods.

Low fat cooking	**high fat cooking**
Cooked in its own juices	deep fried
Poached	Fried
Broiled	Cream sauce
Baked	Buttered sauce

Barbeque   Cheese sauce
Grilled   Sautéed
Roasted   Sweet and sour
                Plum sauce

How we know if we are Diabetic or not?

One thing is about to know exactly our exact ideal body weight, Body Mass Index (BMI) especially the kilocalorie intake affect to our ideal weight because if your BMI under 18 is slim, 20-25 is normal, 25 to 30 is overweight and higher than 30 is obese. This is the formula to know exactly your Body Mass Index (BMI).

Formula for BMI:

1. Multiply your weight (pounds) x 703=

2. The result divide into your height (inches)

3. The result from the number step 2 to divide again into your height inches= your BMI

For example:

1. 160lbsx703=112,480

2. 112,480/Height 68"inches (conversion of 5'8" ft.)=1,654.11765

3. 1,654.11765/Height 68"inches (conversion of 5'8"ft)=24.32 BMI result

Leftover Foods

Table for converting inches to feet

Conversion of 1 foot to inches= 12 inches

Inches = Feet	Inches = Feet	Inches = Feet	Inches = Feet	Inches = Feet
12" = 1'0"	24" = 2'0"	36" = 3'0"	48" = 4'0"	60" = 5'0"
13" = 1'1"	25" = 2'1"	37" = 3'1"	49" = 4'1"	61" = 5'1"
14" = 1'2"	26" = 2'2"	38" = 3'2"	50" = 4'2"	62" = 5'2"
15" = 1'3"	27" = 2'3"	39" = 3'3"	51" = 4'3"	63" = 5'3"
16" = 1'4"	28" = 2'4"	40" = 3'4"	52" = 4'4"	64" = 5'4"
17" = 1'5"	29" = 2'5"	41" = 3'5"	53" = 4'5"	65" = 5'5"
18" = 1'6"	30" = 2'6"	42" = 3'6"	54" = 4'6"	66" = 5'6"
19" = 1'7"	31" = 2'7"	43" = 3'7"	55" = 4'7"	67" = 5'7"
20" = 1'8"	32" = 2'8"	44" = 3'8"	56" = 4'8"	68" = 5'8"
21" = 1'9"	33" = 2'9"	45" = 3'9"	57" = 4'9"	69" = 5'9"
22" = 1'10"	34" = 2'10"	46" = 3'10"	58" = 4'10"	70" = 5'10"
23" = 1'11"	35" = 2'11"	47" = 3'11"	59" = 4'11"	71" = 5'11"

Weight-Height charts

Conversion of 1 Kilograms (kg) to Pounds (lbs.) = 2.21 lbs.
Lbs.: 100 105 110 115 120 125 130 135 140 145 150 155 165

Weight
Kgs.: 45.5 47.7 50.0 52.3 54.5 56.8 59.1 61.4 63.6 65.9 68.2 70.5 72.7

WOMEN Height Frame Size in Pounds			
Ft. In.	Small	Medium	Large
4'10"	102-111	109-121	118-131
4'11"	103-113	111-123	120-134
5'0"	104-115	113-126	122-137
5'1"	106-118	115-129	125-140
5'2"	108-121	118-132	128-143
5'3"	111-124	121-135	131-147
5'4"	114-127	124-138	134-151
5'5"	117-130	127-141	137-155
5'6"	120-133	130-144	140-159
5'7"	123-136	133-144	143-163
5'8"	126-139	136-150	146-167
5'9"	129-142	139-153	149-170
5'10"	132-145	142-156	152-173
5'11"	135-148	145-159	155-176
6'0"	138-151	148-162	158-176

Leftover Foods

MEN
Height Frame Size in Pounds

Ft. In	Small	Medium	Large
5'2"	128-134	131-141	138-150
5'3"	130-136	133-143	140-153
5'4"	132-138	135-145	142-156
5'5"	134-140	137-148	144-160
5'6"	136-142	139-151	146-164
5'7"	138-145	142-154	149-168
5'8"	140-148	145-157	152-172
5'9"	142-151	156-160	155-176
5'10"	144-154	151-163	158-180
5'11"	146-157	154-166	161-184
6'0"	143-160	157-170	164-188
6'1"	152-164	160-174	168-192
6'2"	155-168	165-178	172-197
6'3"	158-172	167-182	176-202
6'4"	162-176	171-187	181-207

Some Useful Information

Avocado – *(Persea Americana)* is a pear-shaped fruit with a rough leathery skin, smooth oily edible flesh, and a large seed. It is also called ALLIGATOR PEAR. It is a tree native to Puebla Mexico and Central America and refers to the fruit, botanically a large berry that contains a single seed.[7]

Butter – is a dairy product – a pale yellow edible fatty substance made by churning fresh or fermented cream or milk. It is used as a spread or in cooking. The word is also commonly used to describe puréed vegetable or seed and nut products such as peanut butter and almond butter.

Coriander / Chinese parsley / Cilantro / Culantro – *(Coriandrum sativum)* different names for the same plant. The leaves are considered an herb. The seeds – Coriander – are considered a spice, which contains phytochemicals that may delay or prevent the spoilage of food prepared with it. The fresh leaves and dried seeds are edible and the leaves are variously referred to as coriander leaves, fresh coriander, Chinese parsley or in North America they are called Cilantro.

Eggplant – *(Solanum melongena)* the large egg-shaped fruit of an old world plant, eaten as a vegetable. Its skin is typically dark purple, but the skin of certain cultivated varieties is white or yellow. Commonly known in British English as ***aubergine*** (its name in French) and also known as ***melongen, garden egg or guinea squash.***[8]

Lemon – *(Citrus limon, family Rutaceae)* is a yellow, oval citrus fruit with thick skin and fragrant, acidic juice. It is a small evergreen tree native to Asia. Lemon rind, juice and zest are used in a wide variety of foods and drinks.

> **Lemon juice** is used to make lemonade, soft drinks, and cocktails. It is used in marinades for fish, where its acid neutralizes amines in fish by converting them into nonvolatile

---

7   Wikipedia. www.en.wikipedia.org/wiki/Avocado.

8   Oregon State University. http://food.oregonstate.edu/glossary/eggplant.html

ammonium salts, and meat, where the acid partially hydrolyzes tough collagen fibers, tenderizing the meat, but the low pH denatures the proteins, causing them to dry out when cooked.[9]

Lemon is very useful especially for our health. I've been experimenting using lemon juice combined with my 1.5 liters of water. I haven't had the flu or a cold when everybody else gets sick at home. If you are acidic limit your lemon intake.

Olive oil – *(fruit of Olea europaea, family Oleaceae)* is oil pressed from ripe olives, used in cooking, medicine, soap, etc. pressing whole olives produces the oil. There are different classifications in commercial grades of oil. In countries that adhere to the standard from IOC (International Olive Council), as well as in Australia, and under voluntary USDA labeling standards in the United States:

> ***Extra-virgin olive oil*** – is the highest quality and most expensive olive oil classification. It has superior taste and can be defined as having no sensory defects. It should smell and taste like fresh olives. Extra-virgin oil accounts for less than 10% in many producing countries; the percentage is far higher in the Mediterranean (Greece 80%, Italy 65% and Spain 30%). The fatty acids and antioxidants in extra-virgin olive oil have some powerful health benefits, including a reduced risk of heart disease.
>
> ***Virgin olive oil*** – comes from virgin production only and means produced without mechanical treatment. Virgin olive oil – a production from virgin oil but slightly lower quality with free acidity of up to 1.5% and judged a good taste.
>
> ***Refined olive oil*** – Means strong taste because it is chemically treated to neutralize the acid content to be free of fatty acids, including the grade extra-virgin olive oil and virgin olive oil that can't contain any refined oil is the olive oil

---

9   Wikipedia. http://en.wikipedia.org/wiki/Lemon

obtained from virgin olive oils by refining methods that do not lead to alterations in the initial glyceride structure? It has a free acidity; expressed as oleic acid, of no more than 0.3 grams per 100 grams (0.3%) and its other characteristics correspond to those fixed for this category in the IOC standards. According to the IOC, 50 percent of the oil produced in the Mediterranean requires refining to make it suitable for human consumption from a taste perspective. [10]

Olive pomace oil – means using solvents to extract from pomace this is a type of process blending pomace olive oil with some virgin oil. It is considered good for consumption including restaurants and home cooking because it has the same fat composition as regular olive oil and gives the same health benefits. Pomace means (especially in cider making) the pulpy residue remaining after fruit has been crushed in order to extract its juice. The pulpy matter remaining after some other substance has been pressed or crushed, for example castor oil seeds after the oil has been extracted. [11]

Lampante virgin olive oil – Is the lowest grade of virgin olive oil and is not fit for human consumption without further refinement. It is the product of poor processing or poor fruit and is produced mechanically. In Italy it refers to an oil lamp and is used for industrial purposes or refined to make it edible.

Onion – *[Allium cepa, family liliaceae (or alliaceae)]* is an edible bulb with a pungent taste and smell composed of several concentric layers, used in cooking. The plant that produces the onion, with long rolled or strap-like leaves and spherical heads of garnish-white flowers. Known as bulb onion

---

10   International Olive Council: www.oliveoilsource.com/definition/refined-olive-oil

11   Oxford Dictionaries: http://www.oxforddictionaries.com/

or common onion it is used as a vegetable and is the most widely cultivated species of the genus allium.[12]

Sea salt – is derived through the evaporation of seawater. The difference between iodized and table salt and sea salt is that it never undergoes processing and is pure with no additives. The levels of minerals, like potassium, calcium and other nutrients remain complete.

Table salt and iodized salt come from salt deposits that are then processed to a fine texture making it easier to use in cooking cakes and other baking recipes. During processing, additives such as iodine are included.

Your consumption of any kind of salt should be limited to 1200-1500 mg per day. One teaspoon of salt is equivalent to 1300 mg sodium. The recipes in this book rarely call for salt and some with just a pinch because too much salt is not healthy.

Sweet Potatoes – (*Convolvulaceae*) are an edible tropical tuber with pinkish-orange slightly sweet flesh and is a dicotyledonous plant. The leaves can be eaten too and are used in cooking especially salads. It is rich in complex carbohydrates, dietary fiber and beta-carotene (a provitamin A), carotenoid and moderate contents of other micronutrients including vitamin B5, vitamin B6, manganese and potassium. [13]

When baked by cooking small changes in variables occur in micronutrient content occurs to include a higher content of vitamin C at 24% of the Daily Value per 100 gm. serving as well as an increase in polyphenol levels. [14]

What About Tapioca Flour and Starch?

Tapioca comes from the cassava roots. It is grated then squeezed completely all the white milky liquid is removed. Then dried for one hour until it is a white powder like starch. It is a gluten free substitution for your

---

12   Wikipedia: http://en.wikipedia.org/wiki/Onion

13   Wikipedia. http://en.wikipedia.org/wiki/Sweet_potato

14   Ibid.

bread or food mix. Also used to enhance the texture and taste of your baked goods. It can also be used to thicken sauces and gravies.

It is more malleable than cornstarch and gives cookies and cakes a chewy or crispy texture.

Where I grew up, we always loved to make a variety of foods using tapioca. I will share this with you in my next book containing my secret ways of cooking using tapioca and how to make perfect tasty dishes.

What is Cassava Rice?

Extracted from the tapioca making procedures, having a natural sour smell, the leftover pieces become cassava rice. It has a wide range of use since it is gluten free and can be a substitute to wheat like paleo diet, macrobiotic diet, gluten free diet and diabetic diet can use it as a substitution to gluten. You can use it in steamed bread and steamed cake making and it very easy to cook by adding or combining other ingredients. It is excellent as a replacement for eggs, milk or any dairy products.

Cassava Rice Can Be a Substitute of Rice

Cassava rice in my own perception and from experimentations that it can be a substitute. To any types of grains and rice because nowadays a rising number of the population are trying to avoid rice especially the white rice because of change of living by switching to healthier diets like Paleo diets, Macrobiotic diets, Diabetic diets and more people in fitness programs embrace those diets to avoid starches from rice that filled with minerals without any micronutrients.

What is Rice?

It is one of the grain family and it is used widely as a staple food by a large population. Grown in the tropical countries and according to Wikipedia rice is ranked third for worldwide, production and consumption after sugarcane and maize.

What is Glycemic Index?

In my own understanding glycemic index is a type of carbohydrates that when is formed into a sugar then it affects our blood glucose or blood sugar, that can cause people to become diabetics. Examples of foods that use a lot of Glycemic Index (GI) are mostly processed candies, some BBQ sauces, crystal powder drinks, carbonated drinks like sodas and certain sauces.

What is Arsenic?

According to my research that **Arsenic** can be found in the soil and it comes from the minerals that contents toxins. Organic foods made from rice or wheat cereals contain a higher level of arsenic. in my country of the Philippines where I grew up and mostly of Asia.

The main staple food is white rice; My Great-grandmother when she prepared rice for cooking she rubbed all the uncooked rice many times between her hands while soaking it in water, then she would change the water at least 5 times during the rubbing process until the water had no more white tint was showing, then she would measure the leftover clear water then use it for cooking together with the rice.

In my research, I found out that arsenic is the main cause in countries having related issues with organic wheat food containing toxins. A large number of people are getting seriously sick and some organic baby food that have mostly the highest contamination by arsenic.

Guidelines and Illustrations

Learning to use your leftover foods to create tasty new meals may mean creating new habits. This chapter will give you some ideas on how to approach your leftover foods with new creativity. The idea is to save you some time, put healthy meals together and avoid wasting any food. The goal is to give you more time to do other things without missing out on any meals or nutritious snacks.

Why is Leftover Food Essential?

Working with leftover food gives you more options with your foods and meals:

- it saves time;
- it's convenient (you are at home in your own kitchen);
- you can experiment with tastes and flavors;
- you can avoid processed spices, condiments and sauces that could harm your health when consumed too often.

Looking at the chart about leftover food essentials, you can see that using leftover foods is win-win for you, your family, your friends and your community (less waste, less garbage, better for the environment).

What Are the Essentials of Leftover Foods?

Breakfast, Brunch, Lunch, and Dinner, including packed lunches/ meals and emergency food.

BREAKFAST – A meal eaten in the morning, the first of the day. Traditional breakfasts include toast, eggs, sausages, a cup of tea, coffee, hot chocolate or milk. This book will give you different ideas for using leftover foods at breakfast so that you can save without wasting.

The important thing to remember before cooking another fresh meal is what leftover food you have that could be turned into a quick, nutritious breakfast. If you have limited time and need to get to work, school or other activities then a breakfast using leftover food could be the answer.

BRUNCH – A late morning meal eaten instead of breakfast and lunch. It was first coined in the late 19th century by some British students (probably after a late night out Saturday). Brunch has taken on a life of its own and can include everything from breakfast dishes to dinner dishes and everything in between. In your kitchen, it can include all kinds of leftover foods depending on your time and energy.

LUNCH – The meal eaten in the middle of the day, typically one that is lighter or less formal than an evening meal, although that is changing as many people turn to lighter suppers. It sometimes depends of your appetite whether you feel like eating a salad, BBQ rolled wrapped salad. Traditionally in my home, the meals we prepare for lunch are a little bit heavier than breakfast.

Others follow the advice:
    Breakfast – eat like a King
    Lunch – eat like a prince
    Supper – eat like a pauper (very light)

DINNER – The main meal of the day, taken either around midday or in the evening. A traditional supper would include awesome foods like BBQ steak, grilled salmon, Kebabs, and we usually have dessert. Sometimes supper time is buffet style.

PACK LUNCH OR PACK MEALS – Usually for people who go to work or school away from home without a free meal. People take homemade to save money by not buying from a food court or cafeteria or a restaurant. You can have a healthy meal if you plan ahead.

EMERGENCY FOOD – Everybody has something in their fridge that's an emergency food so when they're hungry or don't have time to cook a meal they depend on the saved food. My next-door neighbor told me this book is a good idea. They are retired yet time goes by so fast and what they really need are some ideas to prepare for their meals.

Leftover Foods Recipe Guide

Below is a Leftover Foods Guide for you to look up my sample recipes for some ideas for breakfast, brunch, lunch, dinner for a change from traditionally to a modern way including halal, gluten free, Kosher and vegetarian. Each recipe gives optional and substitutable ingredients as well seasonal guides for recipes for spring, summer, fall/autumn and winter all tasted/ tested as well.

BREAKFAST

1. Hot rice arroz caldo
2. Feast wrap
3. Egg sandwich
4. Pan de sal de Mexican fajitas
5. Pan de sal Bavarian German
6. Pan de sal de Pilipinas adobo
7. Pan de sal de Queso
8. Pan de sal de Vegetarian

BRUNCH

1. Fresh rolled salad/avocado
2. Colored coding bell pepper
3. Nasi Lemak modern style
4. Brunch leftover bread
5. Brunch baked sushi mini cupcakes
6. Feast wrap
7. Pan de sal de Mexico fajitas
8. Pan de sal de Queso
9. Pan de sal Bavaria Germany
10. Pan de sal de Pilipinas adobo
11. Pan de sal de vegetarian
12. Egg sandwich
13. Fruit cocktail Quesadillas

LUNCH

1. Vegetable soup with macaroni
2. Hot carrots soup
3. Wrapped leftover foods
4. French onion soup
5. Pan de sal de Mexican fajitas
6. Pan de sal de Pilipinas adobo
7. Pan de sal de Queso (Cheese bread)
8. Baked salmon
9. Pan de sal de Bavaria Germany
10. Pan de sal de Vegetarian
11. Fruit cocktail Quesadillas

DINNER

1. Guacamole
2. Guacamole appetizer
3. Onion gravy with crackers
4. Stir-fried spaghetti
5. Fried rice with vegetable
6. Chocolate fondue
7. Chucky sweet potatoes
8. Potatoes with sour cream
9. French onion soup
10. Pan de sal de Queso (Cheese bread)
11. Pan de sal de Mexican fajitas
12. Pan de sal de Pilipinas adobo
13. Pan de sal Bavaria Germany
14. Baked salmon
15. Pan de sal de Vegetarian
16. Cheese fondue with leftover Bread

PACK LUNCH OR PACK MEALS

1. Fresh rolled salad with fresh avocado
2. Nasi lemak modern style (Malaysian food)
3. Wrapped leftover foods
4. Fried rice with vegetable
5. Feast wrap
6. Pan de sal de Mexican fajitas
7. Pan de sal de Queso
8. Pan de sal de Pilipinas adobo
9. Pan de sal Bavaria Germany
10. Pan de sal de Vegetarian

EMERGENCY FOOD

Leftovers are a source when you need to have quick and fast yet healthy food. Some examples of leftover foods that we can call *Emergency Food* include:

> Barbequed/grilled meats, vegetables and fish
> Cooked rice
> Cooked eggs
> Cooked potatoes
> Ripe fruits

To avoid food poisoning, ensure the leftovers are properly packaged and labeled with the date stored. Many cooked leftovers will last up to a week in the fridge, although it's best to do a smell test and visual for any discoloration.

Seasonal Guide

Spring – The season after winter and before summer, in which vegetation begins to appear – in the northern hemisphere from March to May and in the southern hemisphere from September to November.[15]

Summer – The warmest season of the year – in the northern hemisphere from June to August and in the southern hemisphere from December to February.[16]

Autumn/Fall – The third of the year when crops and fruits are gathered and leaves fall – in the northern hemisphere from September to November and in the southern hemisphere from March to May.[17]

Winter – The coldest season of the year – in the northern hemisphere from December to March and in the southern hemisphere from June to August.[18] Fruits and vegetables in winter ripen late in the growing season and are suitable for storage over the winter, like a winter apple. Wheat or other crops in winter are sown in autumn for harvesting the following year.

Bottom line: the entire recipe guide here is for all seasons: spring, summer, fall/autumn and winter.

---

15   Google: https://www.google.ca/#q=define+spring

16   Google: https://www.google.ca/#q=define+Summer+

17   Google: https://www.google.ca/#q=define+autumn

18   Google: https://www.google.ca/#q=define+winter

Recipes for Spring, Summer, Fall and Winter

5-10 minutes

1. Fresh rolled salad with fresh avocado - 5 minutes
2. Hot carrots soup – 5 minutes
3. Guacamole – 5 minutes
4. Guacamole appetizer – 5 minutes
5. Onion gravy with crackers – 6 minutes
6. Colored coding bell pepper – 8 minutes
7. Nasi lemak modern style (Malaysian food) – 10 minutes
8. Dry vegetable adobo – 6 minutes
9. Brunch leftover bread – 3 minutes
10. Stir-fried spaghetti – 10 minutes
11. Fried rice with vegetables – 7 minutes
12. Chocolate fondue – 5 minutes.
13. Brunch baked sushi mini cupcakes - 7 minutes
14. Chunky creamy sweet potatoes – 5 minutes
15. Hot rice arroz caldo – 7 minutes
16. Potato with sour cream – 3 minutes
17. Feast wrap – 3 minutes
18. Egg sandwich – 4 minutes
19. Mexican wrapped taco – 7 minutes
20. Fruit cocktail Quesadillas – 6 minutes
21. Cheese fondue with leftover bread – 8 minutes

Leftover Foods

10-25 minutes

1. Vegetable soup – 12 minutes
2. Wrapped leftover foods – 12 minutes
3. Baked salmon – 12 minutes

1 hour – 4 hours

1. Pan de sal de Mexico fajitas – 3 hours
2. Pan de sal de Pilipinas adobo– 3 hours
3. Pan de sal de Queso (Cheese bread) – 3 hours
4. Pan de sal Bavaria Germany – 3 hours
5. Pan de sal de Vegetarian – 3 hours

Leftover Foods that are Easy to Save

Fridge: 10 days
Freezer: 15-20 days
Barbequed meats
Barbequed vegetables
Cooked rice
Cooked pasta
Dried cooked meats
Barbequed fish fillets
Dried cooked fish fillets
Dried cooked vegetables
Grilled meats
Grilled vegetables
Grilled fish
Breads
Ripe fruits
Dried foods
Broth-based soups[19]*
Cream soups: Two days with milk (including coconut milk) or cream*

---

19 * Most soups freeze well up to six months.

Yogurt Storage

Open containers of yogurt last 4 days

Eggs

Fried eggs: Up to four days in the fridge
Hard-boiled eggs with shells intact: Up to seven days
Peeled hard-boiled eggs: Up to five days. To save cracked fresh eggs don't leave them in the shells. All you need to do is to: Place the eggs in a bowl; beat the eggs for 5 strokes only. Pour the content in as many ice cube trays as needed then put the trays In a freezer. Recommend seal wrap or ziploc bags the trays. To avoid freezer burns or freezer taste.

Leftover Food Targets for Health

Our bodies need six main nutrients every day: carbohydrates, protein, vitamins, fats, minerals and water.

Carbohydrate – Any of the large group of organic compounds occurring in the foods and living tissues and including sugars, starch and cellulose. They contain hydrogen and oxygen in the same ratio as water (2:1) and typically can be broken down to release energy in the animal body.[20]

Protein – Any of a class of nitrogenous organic compounds that consist of the large molecules composed of one or more long chains of amino acids and are an essential part of all living organisms, especially as a structural component of body tissues such as muscle, hair, collagen, etc., and as enzymes and antibodies. [21]

Vitamins – Any of a group of organic compounds that is essential for normal growth and nutrition and are required in small quantities in the diet because they cannot be synthesized by the body.[22]

---

20   Oxford Dictionaries: www.oxforddictionaries.com/definition/english/carbohydrate.

21   Ibid: www.oxforddictionaries.com/definition/english/protein.

22   Ibid: www.oxforddictionaries.com/definition/english/vitamin.

Leftover Foods

Minerals – Inorganic substances needed by the human body for good health.[23]

Fats – A fatty substance made from animals or plant products, used in cooking. Chemistry definition: Any group or natural esters of glycerol and various fatty acids, which are solid at room temperature and are the main constituents of animal and vegetable fats.[24]

Water – A colorless, transparent, odorless, tasteless liquid that forms the seas, lakes, rivers, and rain and is the basis of the fluids of living organisms.[25]

Why Did I Make This Chart for Leftover Foods Only?

The preparation, storage and handling of leftover foods are part of our daily healthy lifestyle. We need to be careful how we make and cook our food. Food poisoning is no fun and it can kill. So this is why we always make sure that we are handling and cooking food properly. When you buy fast food or takeout, you can't see how that food has been handled or what additives have been put in.

Before planning any meal, it is important to know the nutritional value of the dish. Leftover foods should aim to preserve all of the nutrients while making another creative meal. You should know exactly what ingredients are being used and educate yourself about them. Make it part of your healthy lifestyle to know what ingredients are good for you and which ones you can substitute with a healthier choice.

Some people think the obesity epidemic is caused by leftover foods. Not True! Obesity comes from having too many carbohydrates and sugars in food and then eating portion sizes that are too large. Add in sugar-laden sodas and fat/sugar/salt-laden snacks and you have a recipe for obesity.

According to the Trust for America's Health, adult obesity rates have doubled since 1980 – from 15 percent to 30 percent. Childhood obesity rates have tripled over the same period. "Nearly one out of three children and teens ages 2 to 19 is overweight or obese."[26]

---

23   Ibid: www.oxforddictionaries.com/definition/english/mineral.

24   Ibid: www.oxforddictionaries.com/definition/english/fat.

25   Ibid: www.oxforddictionaries.com/definition/english/water.

26   Trust for America's Health. *The State of Obesity: Better Policies for a Healthier America.*

Pan de sal Bread Dough

(Optional and Substitutable Ingredients)

Ingredients:
---

6 cups King Arthur White whole-wheat flour unbleached (Substitutable)

2½-teaspoon active dry yeast dissolved in 2 cups warm water. Let stand for 4 minutes or until it bubbles

½ cup brown sugar

Pinch of sea salt
125grams / 1 stick softened salted butter

Breadcrumbs

1. To 3 cups of the flour from the ingredients add salt, sugar and mix well with wooden spoon.

2. Add the softened butter, pour yeast mixture into the floured mixture and mix slowly using the wooden spoon. Add the remaining 3 cups of flour and mix well then mix again using your hands or machine (If using a machine, for the last part always use your hands to finished kneading and then pour onto the floured kneading surface.)

3. Form a ball and then knead for 5 minutes or until it become smooth and soft then form a ball.

(September 2014) http://healthyamericans.org/report/115.

4. Place in a large mixing bowl and cover with a clean cloth. Leave to rise for 1½ hours or until it doubles in size.

5. After the dough has risen, remove it from the mixing bowl and on the kneading surface form small round but not perfectly round (You can put the fillings in and close or sealed) and roll the balls in breadcrumbs. Do the same with the rest of the dough others then place on a baking sheet, cover and let it rise for about 1-½ hours. Twenty minutes ahead, preheat the oven to 375°F.

6. Bake the pan de sal for 7-8 minutes or until they become golden brown.

7. Serve hot.

Pan de sal Bread Dough (Optional and Substitutable Ingredients)

How To Make Cassava Rice

(Sweet Potato Rice and Taro Rice)

(Optional and Substitutable Ingredients)

Ingredients:

3 Cups Fresh Grated cassava root

Equipment:
Grater (zest grater)
White clean cloth
Big sheet pan or flat bread baking pan
Medium bowl

1. Put 1 cup of the grated cassava root in the clean white cloth and squeeze out the liquid to separate the starchy water. Then if all the liquid is removed, place the Cassava into the flat baking pan and then spread the content using your fingers until it turns into crumbs.

2. Leave for 2 to 3 hours uncovered, until it dry. If you want to save in a Ziploc or containers let it dry longer on your counter for about 3 to 48 hours uncovered but if you have a sunny and hot day you can dry this under the sun and then when it is totally dry, you can save it using Ziploc bags or a container.

Cauliflower Rice

---- **Ingredients:** ----

1 whole fresh cauliflower
1 tsp. olive oil
Pinch of Celtic sea salt (optional and substitutable)

Equipment:
Electric food processor (optional)

Manual Medium grater or cheese grater (Substitute if you don't have food processor)

Frying pan

Wooden spoon

Knife

Ziploc or Baggies

1. **Wash the cauliflower; Make sure no brown or black spots. Cut the core in the bottom to removed all the green stem and then break the florist of each connected to the core any own size.**

2. **Put by batches into the food processor (if you using a food processor) until it chopped but not like a pulverized. If you using grater grate each one of the pieces.**

3. Preheat frying pan and spread the olive oil and then pour the 1-½ Cups of cauliflower rice. Stir for 3 minutes until it dried up.

4. Continue until it's all done and remove all in to the bowl and divided each bag you wanted to have the amount and sealed it tight without air inside the bag then put in your freezer.

Tips and advice:
If the cauliflower rice is frozen, leave in your counter until it defrost by itself then ready to use for cooking.

How To Make Liquid Stocks

(Optional and Substitutable Ingredients)

Ingredients:

½ Kilo raw chicken carcasses medium dice chopped (Substitutable)

2 bay leaves

1 medium carrots medium dice chopped

¼ head garlic unpeeled

2 liters cold water

1 medium onions 1 medium leek medium dice chopped

2 stick celery medium dice chopped

2 sprigs fresh parsley

2 whole black peppercorns

1. **Pour cold water into the Medium size of saucepan, add all ingredients and bring to boil for 5 minutes in a moderate heat.**

2. **Pass the stock into the fine sieve. Let it cool down for at least half hour. Then refrigerate. Keep it for 4 to 5 days in your fridge. But freezing point around 2 to 3 months. Do not throw the meats.**

How To Make Almond Flour

Ingredients:

Almond peeled or Blanched almond peeled

Equipment:

Electric food processor (or manual grinder to ground the almond)

Spatula or rubber scraper

Medium size Ziploc or Containers with lids

1. **If the almond still not blanched, you blanched this and then peel to disregards the skin.**
2. **Pour in to the food processor and grind until it become fine.**
3. **Transfer to a Ziploc or container to save your almond flour.**

How To Make Breads Dough

For Paleo Diet, Gluten Free Diet, Diabetic, Macrobiotic Diet, Vegetarian, Halal Or Kosher

Ingredients:

1-cup cassava rice

1-cup coconut flour

¼ cup flaxseeds meal Golden should be fine
½ cup almond flour (optional)

6 pieces eggs (optional and substitutable) if you don't use eggs 1 cups coconut milk sweetened or unsweetened

1 teaspoon Baking soda

1 cup fresh coconut juice (substitutable) if you don't have fine with 1 cup warmed water

2 Tablespoon apple ciders

¼ Teaspoon sea salt

8-tablespoon extra light olive oil

1. **Preheat oven 360 F.**
2. **Beat eggs and combine all liquid into a separate bowl then blend together.**
3. **Blend all dry ingredients and then pour all liquid mixtures into the floured mixtures.**
4. **Pour into the loaf pan and baked for about 1 hour or until become golden brown.**
5. **Removed from the oven and let it cools down for about 15 minutes before slicing.**

Two Way of Cooking The Cassava Rice

(With Liquids or Without Liquid)

It is better to steam the Cassava rice rather than bake it in dry heat and you can put the fillings for both with liquids or without liquids like Pan de sal buns filling with or without liquids

With Liquids

Ingredients:

3 cups Cassava rice (Do not squeeze out the liquid starch of fresh grated cassava)
Banana leave or Greased wax paper
1/8 cup brown sugar (optional and substitutable)

1. **Preheat steamer in medium heat.**

2. **Combine all ingredients in the mixing bowl and then mix until well blended to a unformed texture.**

3. **Form into a ball or whatever shape you like. Wrap and seal both sides of the wrapper.**

4. **Put in the steamer and steam for 20 to 25 minutes or until fully cooked.**

5. **Let it cool down for 10 minutes and serve and enjoy.**

Without Liquids

Ingredients:
---

2 cups cassava rice
½ cup fresh grated coconut.
¼ cup brown sugar

1. **Preheat the steamer.**

2. **Mix all the ingredients and then pour into a small single medium size steaming bowl or glass baking bowl or Pyrex medium size bowl. You can put the filling between the half of the mixtures before you pour the other half.**

3. **Cover with cotton cloth and seal and then steam in about 30-35 minutes or until stick together and smooth.**

4. **Cool down for 10 minutes and serve.**

Tips:
You can put fillings each of the rolled cassava rice mixtures. with liquids or without liquids.

Food Preparation Time Guide

5-10 minutes

1. Fresh rolled salads with fresh avocado - 5 minutes
2. Hot carrots soup – 5 minutes
3. Guacamole – 5 minutes
4. Guacamole appetizer – 5 minutes
5. Onion gravy with crackers 6 minutes
6. Colored coding bell pepper – 8 minutes
7. Nasi lemak modern style (Malaysian food) – 10 minutes
8. Dry vegetable adobo – 6 minutes
9. How to saved leftover fresh avocado – 2 minutes
10. Brunch leftover bread – 3 minutes
11. Stir-fried spaghetti – 10 minutes
12. Fried rice with vegetables – 7 minutes
13. Chocolate fondue – 5 minutes
14. Brunch baked sushi mini cupcakes -7 minutes
15. Chunky creamy sweet potatoes – 5 minutes
16. Hot rice arro'z caldo – 7 minutes
17. Potato with sour cream – 3 minutes

18. Feast wrap – 3 minutes

19. Egg sandwich – 4 minutes

20. Mexican wrapped taco – 7 minutes

21. Fruit cocktail Quesadillas – 6 minutes

22. Cheese fondue with leftover bread – 8 minutes

10-25 minutes

1. Vegetable soup – 12 minutes
2. Wrapped leftover foods – 12 minutes
3. Baked salmon – 12 minutes.
4. French onion – 15 minutes

1 hour – 4 hours

1. Pan de sal de mexico fajitas – 3 hours
2. Pan de sal de Pilipinas adobo – 3 hours
3. Pan de sal de Queso (Cheese bread) – 3 hours
4. Pan de sal Bavaria Germany – 3 hours
5. Pan de sal de vegetarian– 3 hours

Leftover Food Recipes

Optional and Substitutable Ingredients

"Your choices and decision might always good for you health in the end so be aware to know the best for you"

You are	Who can eat?	You can't eat (Optional)	Substitution
Gluten free non-celiac Sensitivity	✔	Crabstick imitation Peanut Satay sauce	Gluten free salad dressing
Halal	✔	Crabstick imitation, Non-Halal Meat like Pork and duck	Halal meat like lamb, beef and chicken, vegetables
Kosher	✔	Crabstick imitation, Non-Kosher meat like Pork and duck	Kosher meat like lamb, beef and chicken, Vegetables
Paleo diet	✔	Crabstick imitation, Rice paper wrap	Paleo tortillas made from coconut flour
Macrobiotic diet	✔	Crabstick imitation Meat, Rice paper wrap	Paleo tortillas made from coconut flour, Wheat grains
Fitness Program diet	✔	Crabstick imitation	
Diabetic	✔	Crabstick imitation, rice paper wrap	Paleo tortillas made from coconut flour, Wheat grains
Celiac disease	✔	Crabstick imitation Peanut sauce	Gluten free salad dressing Paleo tortillas made from coconut flour
Vegetarian	✔	Meats from animals Fish Peanut sauce	
Children	✔		

Fresh Rolled Salad with Fresh Avocado

Fresh Rolled Salad with Fresh Avocado

Preparation time: 5 minutes

Leftover Foods: cooked Barbequed meats, barbequed vegetables or as long as dried cooked meat or green salads.

Ingredients:

4 pieces rice paper wrap (available in Asian store and substitutable)

1-cup carrots matchsticks cut or French cut 2 inches
1-cup bean sprouts (optional and substitutable)

1 cup shredded meat or fish (any kind of meat as long as you are allowed to eat from your leftover) (Optional and Substitutable)

4 pieces lettuce – green leaf or Romaine
2 halves of fresh ripe avocado (optional and substitutable)

4 pieces crabstick (optional)
Peanut sauce Satay or salad dressing
(Optional and substitutable)

1. Place the rice paper wrap on a flat plate wider than the wrap.

2. Soak the rice paper wrap in warm water for about 5 seconds only then drain

3. Place the lettuce on top of the soft rice paper wrap and arrange all the ingredients and rolled the lettuce to cover all.

4. Wrap and sealed

5. Serve with dipping sauce or dressing if you don't want to include it with the vegetables inside the rolled wrap.

Reminder:
Everyone can eat this food fresh rolled salad with fresh avocado with your own option and substitution of ingredients if you are;

You are	Who can eat?	You can't eat (Optional)	Substitution
Gluten free non-celiac Sensitivity	✔	Bouillon cubes	Gluten free bouillon cubes
Halal	✔	Pork and Non-halal meat	Halal meat like lamb, beef and chicken
Kosher	✔	Non-kosher meat like pork	Vegetables, Kosher meat
Paleo diet	✔	Processed meat, Potato	Unprocessed meat, carrots
Macrobiotic diet	✔	Meat from animals	Mushroom Cabbage
Fitness Program diet	✔	Potato	Sweet potato, carrots
Diabetic	✔	Potato	Sweet potato, carrots
Celiac disease	✔	Bouillon cubes	Gluten free bouillon cubes
Vegetarian	✔	Meat from animals	Vegetables only
Children	✔		

Hot Carrot Soup with Cabbage

Hot Carrot Soup with Cabbage

Preparation time: 5 minutes

Leftover foods: Cooked potatoes, cooked meat, onion, and carrot

--- **Ingredients:** ---

(the same ingredients on page 42 "How to make liquid stocks) but if you use the stocks you need another 2 liters of water or if you have stocks ready.

Then add the 3 Cups vegetable bouillon cube (optional and substitutable)

3 Cups fresh cabbage cut into Medium square

1. The same direction of "How to make liquid stock" but if you did save the stocks just add all the ingredients above and boil for 5 minutes in medium heat.

Tips: From using the stock to "how to make liquid stocks this is the tips. Do not throw the meats after you take the soup because you can cook again by adding another 2 liters of water and 3 pieces bouillon cubes and 3 cups of cabbage to become **Hot Carrot Soup.**

You are	Who can eat?	You can't eat (Optional)	Substitution
Gluten free non-celiac Sensitivity	✔		
Halal	✔		
Kosher	✔		
Paleo diet	✔		
Macrobiotic diet	✔		
Fitness Program diet	✔		
Diabetic	✔		
Celiac disease	✔		
Vegetarian	✔		
Children	✔	Tons of onions, Ground black pepper	Less onion

Guacamole

Guacamole

Preparation time: 5 minutes

Leftover foods: Very ripe avocado, tomatoes, and onion

---- **Ingredients:** ----

3 whole very ripe avocado
1-tablespoon olive oil
2 tablespoons lemon juice or limejuice
1/8 cup onion or finely - chopped
½ cup finely chopped tomatoes
Pinch of sea salt
Pinch of ground black pepper (optional)

1. **Remove the avocado seed, scoop out the fruit and finely mash using a fork or spatula.**
2. **Combine all remaining ingredients and pour into mashed avocado.**
3. **Serve right away or if you want cold you can put in the fridge for 1 hour then serve.**

   Guacamole is very useful, especially with fajitas, guacamole on crackers or you can use as a dipping sauce for chips.

You are	Who can eat?	You can't eat (Optional)	Substitution
Gluten free non-celiac Sensitivity	✔	Ritz crackers or crackers made by wheat, barley, rye	Rice crackers, Gluten free crackers, Paleo crackers
Halal	✔		
Kosher	✔	Non-kosher Crackers	Ritz crackers
Paleo diet	✔	Ritz crackers or crackers made by wheat, barley, rye Rice crackers	Paleo crackers
Macrobiotic diet	✔	Crackers with animal/dairy ingredients or refined white flour, rice flour Cheese from animals	Nutritious whole grains crackers High fiber crackers, Whole grains crackers, Hig fiber crackers
Fitness Program diet	✔	Ritz crackers or crackers made by refined white flour, white rice flour	High fiber crackers, Paleo crackers, Whole grains crackers, Hig fiber crackers
Diabetic	✔	Ritz crackers or crackers made by refined white flour, white rice flour	High fiber crackers, Paleo crackers, Whole grains crackers, Hig fiber crackers
Celiac disease	✔	Ritz crackers or crackers made by refined white flour	Paleo crackers made by coconut flour, Gluten free crackers
Vegetarianism	✔	Crackers with animal/dairy ingredients Cheese	Ritz crackers Vegetarian cheese
Children	✔		

Guacamole Appetizer

Guacamole Appetizer

Preparation time: 5 minutes

Leftover foods: Guacamole

Ingredients: ---

Guacamole (see previous page for the recipe)
12 pieces Ritz or rice crackers (optional)
½ cup scallion's chives or spring onions finely chopped
3 tablespoon grated cheese (Optional and substitutable)

1. **Place 1 tablespoon of guacamole in the top of the crackers then arrange to the plates.**

2. **Sprinkle chopped chives or spring onion in the top of each Guacamole crackers and the grated cheese.**

3. **Serve while still fresh.**

You are	Who can eat?	You can't eat (Optional)	Substitution
Gluten free non-celiac Sensitivity	✔		
Halal	✔		
Kosher	✔		
Paleo diet	✔		
Macrobiotic diet	✔		
Fitness Program diet	✔		
Diabetic	✔		
Celiac disease	✔		
Vegetarian	✔		
Children	✔		

How to Save Leftover Fresh Avocado

Preparation time: 2 minutes

Leftover foods: Fresh avocado

--- **Ingredients:** ---

Avocado(s) cut in half, seed removed
1 large red onion chopped

1. **Pour all onions and place in the top the avocado then cover. Put in the fridge. It won't turn brown for a day.**

2. **Enjoy!**

    Tip: Too many ripe avocados? Cut into halves lengthwise; Live the seeds much better or even the other half no seeds you can still saved but in time when you need to use the avocado, use first the avocado without seeds because seeds helps avocado to control from drying the fruit. Scoop out the fruit. Lay a bed of chopped red onion in the bottom of a glass container put the avocado over top and seal tightly. Place in the fridge for up to 3 weeks still looking fresh.

You are	Who can eat?	You can't eat (Optional)	Substitution
Gluten free non-celiac Sensitivity	✔	Ritz crackers or crackers made by wheat, barley, rye	Rice crackers, Paleo crackers or High fiber crackers
Halal	✔		
Kosher	✔	Non-kosher Crackers	Certified kosher (e.g. Ritz crackers, Matzos)
Paleo diet	✔	Ritz crackers or crackers made by wheat, barley, rye Rice crackers	Paleo crackers
Macrobiotic diet	✔	Crackers with meat ingredients or refined white flour, rice flour Cheese from animals	Paleo crackers, Whole grains crackers
Fitness Program diet	✔	Ritz crackers or crackers made by refined white flour White rice flour	High fiber crackers, Whole grains crackers, Paleo crackers or High fiber crackers
Diabetic	✔	Ritz crackers or crackers made by refined white flour White rice flour	High fiber/low sodium crackers, Whole grains crackers, Paleo crackers or High fiber crackers
Celiac disease	✔	Ritz crackers or crackers made by wheat, barley, rye	Paleo crackers or High fiber cracker, Rice cracker
Vegetarian	✔	Crackers with meat ingredients Cheese	Ritz crackers Vegetarian cheese
Children	✔	Tons of onions	Less onions

Onion Gravy with Crackers

Onion Gravy with Crackers

Preparation time: 6 minutes

Leftover foods: Onions and gravy.

Ingredients:

¼ cup gravy
¼ cup onions
12 Ritz or rice crackers (Substitutable)
1-tablespoon olive oil
¼ cup fresh parsley finely chopped (Optional)

1. **Heat oil in the frying pan. Sauté onions for 3 minutes.**
2. **Pour gravy into onions and stir for 3 minutes or until onion and gravy mixture thickens.**
3. **Spread on the crackers, arrange on the plate, sprinkle parsley on top and serve.**

You are	Who can eat?	You can't eat (Optional)	Substitution
Gluten free non-celiac Sensitivity	✔		
Halal	✔		
Kosher	✔		
Paleo diet	✔		
Macrobiotic diet	✔		
Fitness Program diet	✔		
Diabetic	✔		
Celiac disease	✔		
Vegetarian	✔		
Children	✔		

Color Coded Bell Pepper

Color Coded Bell Pepper

Preparation time: 8 minutes

Leftover foods: cooked Meats, cooked fish, cheese, bell pepper and other cooked vegetables

Ingredients

1 each yellow, green and orange bell pepper
2 cups Guacamole (see page 57)

1. Cut peppers in half lengthwise and removes the seeds and core. Rinse well.
2. In skillet or non-stick frying pan, grill the whole bell pepper side by side until slightly blackened on each side or becomes soft enough to fold and wait 2 minutes for cooling.
3. Spread out the bell pepper and put 1 tablespoon of filling on each bell pepper and roll up, repeat for the remaining bell peppers and serve.

You can also barbeque the peppers.

You are	Who can eat?	You can't eat (Optional)	Substitution
Gluten free non-celiac Sensitivity	✔		
Halal	✔		
Kosher	✔	Dried prawns, Shrimp paste	Fresh Cucumber
Paleo diet	✔	Rice	Cauliflower rice, Cassava rice, Sweet potato rice, Yam rice and Taro rice See page@@@
Macrobiotic diet	✔	White rice	Cassava rice or cauliflower rice see page @@@
Fitness Program diet	✔	White rice	Cauliflower rice, Cassava rice, Sweet potato rice, Yam rice and Taro rice, (Recipe on page.) Agrave nectar or honey
Diabetic	✔	White rice	Cauliflower rice, Cassava rice, Sweet potato rice, Yam rice and Taro rice, (Recipe on page.) Agrave nectar or honey
Celiac disease	✔		Cassava rice see page @@@
Vegetarian	✔	Dried prawns, shrimp paste	Fresh cucumber
Children	✔	Brown Sugar	Honey, agave nectar

Nasi Lemak Modern Style (Malaysian coconut rice)

Nasi Lemak Modern Style

(Malaysian coconut rice)

Preparation time: 10 minutes

Leftover foods: Cooked steamed rice and hard-boiled eggs

Ingredients:

2 cups cooked rice (leftover foods)

1/8-cup coconut milk

Pinch sea salt to taste

1 medium cucumber

Pandan leaves (not necessary if you can't find it in the supermarket – Substitutable)

Banana leafs for wrapping (Substitutable with baking wax paper)

Side:
Cooked hardboiled eggs

Sweet Sambal (Optional and substitutable sauce)

50 grams / 1.76 oz dried chilies soaked in water to soften, cut in 2-inches pieces

2 shallots

1 teaspoon dried prawn/shrimp paste (Belacan)

2 tablespoons brown sugar

1-tablespoon tamarind pulp mixed with 4 tablespoons water

Pinch of sea salt to taste

4. **Mix together the coconut milk, salt, pandan leaves and the cooked rice in a rice cooker and cook without any water for 10-15 minutes.**

5. **Combine all the ingredients of sweet sambal and blend using electric blender. Heat oil in a medium saucepan over moderate heat and then pour the blended sweet sambal into the heated oil, stir until it becomes thick then remove and let it cool. Set aside.**

6. **Boil the eggs for 16 minutes and drain the water. Peel and cut crosswise ½ inch but if you have leftovers this will not be necessary.**

7. **Place the coconut-cooked rice into a teacup and press. If you have banana leaves you can place the banana leaves on a flat plate and pour the rice from the teacup then place the sweet sambal beside the rice, sliced cucumber and hard-boiled eggs. Serve.**

You are	Who can eat?	You can't eat (Optional)	Substitution
Gluten free non-celiac Sensitivity	✔	Soy sauce with gluten	Gluten free Tamari soy sauce Eggplant, Coconut aminos soy sauce
Halal	✔	Non-Halal meat like Pork and duck	Halal meat like lamb, beef, chicken, Vegetables
Kosher	✔	Non-kosher meats like pork and duck	Vegetables, Kosher meat like lamb, beef and chicken
Paleo diet	✔	Soy sauce with gluten or Soy sauce contains with refined white flour	Gluten free Tamari soy sauce, Coconut aminos soy sauce
Macrobiotic diet	✔	Meats from animals, Soy sauce with gluten or Soy sauce contains with refined white flour	Vegetables
Fitness Program diet	✔	Not too much meat, Soy sauce contains with refined white flour	More vegetables, Gluten free Tamari soy sauce, Coconut aminos soy sauce
Diabetic	✔	Soy sauce contains with refined white flour	Gluten free Tamari soy sauce, Coconut aminos soy sauce
Celiac disease	✔	Soya sauce with wheat	Gluten free Tamari soy sauce, Coconut aminos soy sauce
Vegetarian	✔	Meat from animals	Vegetables
Children	✔	Too much onions	Less onions

Dry Vegetable Adobo

Preparation time: 6 minutes

Leftover foods: Cooked vegetables and cooked meats

Ingredients:

2 cups cooked vegetables julienned cut

2 cups cooked meats small strips (optional and substitutable)

½ cup soy sauce or tamari soy sauce (Gluten free)

¼ cup water

1-tablespoon olive oil

1 medium onion julienned cut
4 cloves garlic finely chopped

1. **Heat the oil in a medium saucepan over moderate heat.**

2. **Sauté garlic and onion for 1 minute and then add meat if you used meats, toss vegetables into the sauté mixture for 2 minutes and then add remaining ingredients. Cover and bring to a boiled until a little bit water remains. Serve.**

You are	Who can eat?	You can't eat (Optional)	Substitution
Gluten free non-celiac Sensitivity	✔	Bread made by wheat like barley, rye and refined white flour	Gluten free bread, paleo bread made from coconut flour, almond flour and cassava rice
Halal	✔		
Kosher	✔	Non-Kosher cheese Non-Kosher butter	2 teaspoon olive oil, Kosher cheese, Kosher butter
Paleo diet	✔	Pita bread made by wheat, Barley, rye, rice, corn and refined white flour	Paleo bread made from coconut flour, almond flour and cassava rice
Macrobiotic diet	✔	Cheese from animals, Butter, Bread from refined white flour, rice flour	2 teaspoon olive oil, Whole grain bread, paleo bread made from coconut flour, almond flour and cassava rice
Fitness Program diet	✔	Made by refined white flour	Gluten free bread
Diabetic	✔	Made by refined white flour	Paleo bread made from coconut flour, almond flour and cassava rice, whole grain bread, Whole grains bread
Celiac disease	✔	Bread made by wheat like barley, rye and refined white flour	Gluten free bread, Paleo bread made from coconut flour, almond flour and cassava rice
Vegetarian	✔	Cheese made from animals Butter made from animals	2 teaspoon olive oil
Children	✔		

Brunch Leftover Bread

Brunch Leftover Bread

Preparation time: 3 minutes

Leftover foods: Bread, Cooked fried eggs like omelet or scrambled eggs

---- **Ingredients:** ----

2 slices White whole wheat bread (substitutable)

1 square cut fried egg the same size as the bread (Substitutable from leftover foods)

2 tablespoons butter

1 slice cheese (optional)

1. Heat a skillet or frying pan over moderate heat, spread the butter on the bread and then place the buttered bread into the heated pan for 45 seconds only.

2. When it turns golden brown flip to the other side, place the cheese on top first then follow with the remaining ingredients.

3. Remove from the pan and serve hot.

You are	Who can eat?	You can't eat (Optional)	Substitution
Gluten free non-celiac Sensitivity	✔	Spaghetti with wheat, Barley and rye	Gluten free Spaghetti or any pasta type, Paleo pasta
Halal	✔	Non-Halal meat like Pork bacon and duck	Halal meat like Lamb, beef, chicken, Vegetables
Kosher	✔	Non-Kosher meat like pork bacon and duck	Vegetables, Kosher meat like Lamb, beef and chickens
Paleo diet	✔	Spaghetti with wheat, Barley, rice, corn and rye	Paleo spaghetti made from sesame seeds flour or almond flour, cassava rice
Macrobiotic diet	✔	Pasta with refined white flour, rice flour	Macrobiotic spaghetti, Paleo spaghetti made from sesame seeds flour or almond flour, cassava rice, Wheat grains pasta
Fitness Program diet	✔	Pasta with refined white flour	High fiber pasta or organic pasta
Diabetic	✔	Pasta with refined white flour	Macrobiotic spaghetti, Paleo spaghetti made from sesame seeds flour or almond flour, cassava rice, Wheat grains pasta
Celiac disease	✔	Spaghetti with wheat, Barley and rye	Gluten free Spaghetti or any pasta type, paleo pasta
Vegetarian	✔		Vegan Spaghetti
Children	✔		

Stir-fried Spaghetti

Preparation time: 10 minutes

Leftover foods: Cooked spaghetti, cooked bacon, cooked vegetables

Ingredients:

Cooked spaghetti (leftover foods)

2 tablespoons olive oil

1 medium red onion or green onion cut lengthwise

Ground pepper to taste (optional)

Sea salt to taste

1 medium sliced zucchini cooked
I small cooked eggplant in slices or cubes (optional and substitutable)

¼ cut cauliflower steam for 5 minutes (optional and substitutable)

Grated cheese (optional)

1-½ cups slice bacon cut into a medium squares

1. **Heat the oil in a medium saucepan over medium heat. Sauté onion for 5 minutes.**
2. **Add vegetables and sauté for 3 minutes to reheat.**
3. **Add steamed cauliflower and mix well.**
4. **Mix in the spaghetti and bacon into the vegetables. Mix well.**
5. **Ready to serve with leftover sauce or a sprinkling of cheese.**

You are	Who can eat?	You can't eat (Optional)	Substitution
Gluten free non-celiac Sensitivity	✔		
Halal	✔	Non-Halal meat like Pork and ducks	Halal meat like Lamb, Beef, Chickens Vegetables
Kosher	✔	Non-Kosher Meat like Pork and ducks	Kosher meat like lamb, beef and chicken
Paleo diet	✔	Rice	Cassava rice, Cauliflower rice and sweet potato rice
Macrobiotic diet	✔	Meat from animals and White rice	
Fitness Program diet	✔	White rice	Cassava rice, Cauliflower rice and sweet potato rice
Diabetic	✔	White rIce	Cassava rice, Cauliflower rice and sweet potato rice
Celiac disease	✔		Cassava rice, Cauliflower rice and sweet potato rice
Vegetarian	✔	Meat from animals	Cassava rice, Cauliflower rice and sweet potato rice
Children	✔	Garlic	

Fried Rice with Vegetables

Fried Rice with Vegetables

Preparation time: 7 minutes

Leftover foods: Cooked rice, cooked meat and cooked vegetables

Ingredients:

2 cups cooked rice (leftover foods)

½ cup cooked meat from leftover foods (optional and substitutable)

½ cup cooked broccoli medium cut

½ cup zucchini medium cut

½ cup cooked cauliflower medium cut

Pinch sea salt to taste

1-tablespoon olive oil

2 cloves garlic finely chopped

1 small red onion finely chopped

¼ cup Garlic finely chopped (optional)

1. **Heat oil in a large saucepan over medium heat, sauté garlic and onions for 1 minute.**

2. **Add rice and salt and sauté for 2 minutes then pour the remaining ingredients on the top and cover. Cook for 3-4 minutes until the vegetables become tender.**

3. **Serve hot.**

You are	Who can eat?	You can't eat (Optional)	Substitution
Gluten free non-celiac Sensitivity	✔	Breads with wheat, barley and rye	Gluten free bread Paleo Bread made from coconut flour, sesame seeds flour, almond flour and cassava rice
Halal	✔		
Kosher	✔		
Paleo diet	✔	Breads with wheat, barley, rice, corn and rye	Paleo bread made from coconut flour, sesame seeds flour, almond flour and cassava rice
Macrobiotic diet	✔	Breads with refined white flour, rice flour	Paleo bread made from coconut flour, sesame seeds flour, almond flour and cassava rice
Fitness Program diet	✔	Breads with refined white flour	Paleo bread made from coconut flour, sesame seeds flour, almond flour and cassava rice
Diabetic	✔	Breads with refined white flour	Paleo bread made from coconut flour, sesame seeds flour, almond flour and cassava rice
Celiac disease	✔	Breads with wheat, barley and rye	Gluten free bread Paleo bread made from coconut flour, sesame seeds flour, almond flour and cassava rice
Vegetarianism	✔		
Children	✔		

Chocolate Fondue

Chocolate Fondue

Preparation time: 5 minutes

Leftover foods: Fruits, sponge cake and breads like mini biscotti

Ingredients:

1-cup leftover fruit like strawberry (Substitutable)

1 cup leftover bread toasted and cut into medium dice (Substitutable)

Fondue sauce:

170 grams / 6 oz. semi-sweet chocolate finely chopped
1-tablespoon corn syrup (optional)
2 tablespoons Amaretto or Grand Marnier (substitutable)
½ cup whipping cream

1. Bring cream in the saucepan to boil and then add the chocolate when it boiling.

2. Stir the cream mixture and the chocolate to mix well together until the chocolate is melted.

3. Pour in the corn syrup and the liqueur then transfer to a fondue pot or a medium glass bowl or ceramic dish to keep the sauce hot and serve immediately.

You are	Who can eat?	You can't eat (Optional)	Substitution
Gluten free non-celiac Sensitivity	✔		Cassava rice, sweet potato rice or vegetable, mashed sweet potato and cauliflower rice
Halal	✔		
Kosher	✔		
Paleo diet	✔	Rice	Cassava rice, sweet potato rice or vegetable, mashed sweet potato and cauliflower rice
Macrobiotic diet	✔	Eggs, Rice	Vegan cheese, Cassava rice, sweet potato rice or vegetable, mashed sweet potato and cauliflower rice
Fitness Program diet	✔	White rice	
Diabetic	✔	White rice	Cassava rice, sweet potato rice or vegetable, mashed sweet potato and cauliflower rice
Celiac disease	✔		Cassava rice, sweet potato rice or vegetable, mashed sweet potato and cauliflower rice
Vegetarian	✔	Eggs	Vegan cheese
Children	✔		

Brunch Baked Sushi Mini Cupcakes

Preparation time: 7 minutes

Leftover foods: Cooked rice, cooked meat and cooked vegetables like eggplants, cooked sweet potato

Ingredients:

2 cups cooked rice

½ cup cooked meat

¼ cup cooked vegetables like zucchini and eggplant finely dice

2 eggs beaten

Pinch of sea salt to taste

1-tablespoon olive oil or vegetable oil

1. Preheat oven 375°F and then grease or butter the cupcake pan. Place and flatten 1 tablespoon of cooked rice into each cupcake mold.

2. Heat oil in a small saucepan and sauté the vegetables and meat for 2 minutes or until softened.

3. Place 1 teaspoon of vegetable and 1 teaspoon of meat on top of the rice in each mold and then pour the egg into the rice, meat and vegetable mixture until mold almost full.

4. Bake for 3- 4 minutes until the eggs are cooked. Turn out of the cupcake mold carefully and serve immediately.

You are	Who can eat?	You can't eat (Optional)	Substitution
Gluten free non-celiac Sensitivity	✔		Gluten free Cream cheese
Halal	✔		
Kosher	✔	Non-Kosher cheese	Kosher cream cheese
Paleo diet	✔		Vegetarian cream cheese
Macrobiotic diet	✔	Cheese from the animals	Vegetarian cream cheese
Fitness Program diet	✔		Vegetarian cream cheese
Diabetic	✔		Regular cheese or Vegetarian cream cheese
Celiac disease	✔		
Vegetarian	✔		Vegetarian cream cheese
Children	✔		

Chunky Creamy Sweet Potatoes

Chunky Creamy Sweet Potatoes

Preparation time: 5 minutes

Leftover foods: Cooked sweet potatoes or cooked potatoes

Ingredients:

1 cooked sweet potato or regular potato preheated
¼ cup cream cheese
2 bunches fresh chives finely chopped
2 tablespoons fresh cilantro or fresh parsley
¼ cup bell pepper finely chopped

1. **Cut potato in half lengthwise, scrape out the middle and mash**

2. **Blend in cream cheese and mix well.**

3. **Sprinkle chives and cilantro on top and serve immediately.**

You are	Who can eat?	You can't eat (Optional)	Substitution
Gluten free non-celiac Sensitivity	✔		Vegetables, Cassava rice, sweet potato rice or cauliflower rice, Regular rice
Halal	✔	Non-Halal meat like Pork and ducks	Halal meat like lamb, beef and chickens Vegetables
Kosher	✔	Non-Kosher meat like Pork and ducks	Kosher meat like lamb, beef and chickens Vegetables
Paleo diet		Rice	Cassava rice, sweet potato rice or cauliflower rice
Macrobiotic diet	✔	Meat from animals like chickens, Rice	Vegetables, Cassava rice, sweet potato rice or cauliflower rice
Fitness Program diet			
Diabetic	✔	White rice	Vegetables, Cassava rice, sweet potato rice or cauliflower rice
Celiac disease	✔	White rice	Vegetables, Cassava rice, sweet potato rice or cauliflower rice, Regular rice
Vegetarian	✔	Meat from animals like Chicken	Vegetables
Children	✔		

Hot Rice Arroz Caldo (Porridge)

Hot Rice Arroz Caldo (Porridge)

Preparation time: 7 minutes

Leftover foods: Cooked rice, cooked meats and cooked vegetables

Ingredients:

2 cups cooked rice

2 big pieces cut up cooked chicken (Optional and substitutable)

4 slices cooked eggplant and cooked zucchini (Optional and substitutable)

Pinch sea salt

1 small green onion or red onion cut into quarters

3 cups water

Combine all ingredients in a medium saucepan, cover and bring to a boil. When at a boil stir slowly until it becomes a little bit thick. Remove and serve hot.

You are	Who can eat?	You can't eat (Optional)	Substitution
Gluten free non-celiac Sensitivity	✔		Gluten free sour cream Paleo sour cream, Sweet potato
Halal	✔		Halal sour cream Gluten free sour cream
Kosher	✔		Kosher sour cream Gluten free sour cream
Paleo diet	✔	Potato	Paleo sour cream Gluten free sour cream, Sweet potato
Macrobiotic diet	✔		Macrobiotic sour cream Gluten free sour cream Paleo sour cream, Sweet potato
Fitness Program diet	✔	Potato	Macrobiotic sour cream Gluten free sour cream Paleo sour cream
Diabetic	✔	Potato	Macrobiotic sour cream Gluten free sour cream Paleo sour cream, Sweet potato
Celiac disease	✔		Macrobiotic sour cream Gluten free sour cream Paleo sour cream, Sweet potato
Vegetarian	✔		Vegetarian sour cream
Children	✔		Sweet potato

Potatoes with Sour Cream

Potatoes with Sour Cream

Preparation Time: 3 minutes

Leftover foods: Peeled cooked potatoes, cooked sweet potato

Ingredients:

2 cups cooked potatoes cut into chunks

3 tablespoons sour cream

½ cup chives or scallions finely chopped

2 tablespoons fresh cilantro or fresh parsley finely chopped

½ cup orange bell pepper diced

½ cup yellow bell pepper diced

Combine all ingredients, mix well and serve immediately.

You are	Who can eat?	You can't eat (Optional)	Substitution
Gluten free non-celiac Sensitivity	✔	Tortillas with wheat, Barley and rye	Corn tortillas Paleo Tortillas
Halal	✔	Non-Halal meat like Pork and ducks	Halal meat like lamb, beef and chickens Vegetables
Kosher	✔	Non-Kosher meat like pork and ducks Mayonnaise	Kosher meat like lamb, beef and chickens Vegetables, Kosher salad dressings
Paleo diet	✔	Tortillas with wheat, Barley, rice, corn and rye	Paleo tortillas made from coconut flour, cassava rice, sweet potato rice, almond flour and sesame seeds flour, Paleo salad dressings
Macrobiotic diet	✔	Meat from animals Mayonnaise, Tortillas made by refined white flour, Rice flour	Vegetables, Paleo Salad dressings, Paleo tortillas made from coconut flour, cassava rice, sweet potato rice, almond flour and sesame seeds flour, whole grain tortillas, corn tortillas
Fitness Program diet	✔	Bread like rice bread and fro refined white flour	Vegetables
Diabetic	✔	Tortillas with refined white flour	Corn tortillas Paleo tortillas made from coconut flour, cassava rice, sweet potato rice, almond flour and sesame seeds flour, whole grain tortillas
Celiac disease	✔	Tortillas with wheat, Barley and rye	Corn tortillas Paleo tortillas made from coconut flour, cassava rice, sweet potato rice, almond flour and sesame seeds flour
Vegetarian	✔	Meat from animals Mayonnaise contain with egg	Vegetables
Children	✔		

Feast Wrap

Feast Wrap

Preparation time: 3 minutes

Leftover foods: Tortillas

Ingredients:

4 small Tortillas White whole wheat or whole wheat (Substitutable)

4 pieces Chicken Ham (Optional and substitutable)

4 leaves green lettuce

½ cup mayonnaise or other salad dressings (Substitutable)

1. Place the lettuce first then the chicken ham and other ingredients onto the middle top of the torilla.
2. Then fold the edge to the middle and continue to roll up to the end.
3. Serve.

You are	Who can eat?	You can't eat (Optional)	Substitution
Gluten free non-celiac Sensitivity	✔	Breads with wheat, barley and rye	Gluten free bread Paleo bread made from coconut flour, cassava rice, sweet potato rice, almond flour and sesame seeds flour
Halal	✔		
Kosher		Non-Kosher eggs	Kosher eggs
Paleo diet	✔	White bread like wheat bread, Rice bread and rye	Paleo bread made from coconut flour, cassava rice, almond flour and sesame seeds flour
Macrobiotic diet	✔	Bread like rice bread and eggs or made fro refined white flour	Paleo bread made from coconut flour, cassava rice, almond flour and sesame seeds flour Wheat grains bread
Fitness Program diet	✔	Breads with like rice bread and fro refined white flour	Gluten free bread Paleo bread
Diabetic	✔	Bread like rice bread and fro refined white flour	Paleo bread made from coconut flour, cassava rice, almond flour and sesame seeds flour Wheat grains
Celiac disease	✔	Breads with wheat, barley and rye	Gluten free bread Paleo bread made from coconut flour, cassava rice, e, almond flour and sesame seeds flour
Vegetarian		Eggs	
Children	✔		

Egg Sandwich

Egg Sandwich

Preparation time: 4 minutes

Leftover foods: Hard-boiled eggs (cooked)

Ingredients:

2 hard-boiled eggs cooked, shells removed
2 slices bread, crust removed (substitutable)
1-tablespoon mayonnaise (substitutable)
½ teaspoon mustard (substitutable)
¼ cup fresh chives finely chopped.

1. **Mash the eggs in a medium bowl. Add all remaining ingredients and mix well.**
2. **Spread the egg mixture on one slice and then cover with the other piece of bread.**
3. **Cut in four.**
4. **Serve right away.**

You are	Who can eat?	You can't eat (Optional)	Substitution
Gluten free non-celiac Sensitivity	✔	Tortillas with wheat, Barley and rye	Corn tortillas Paleo Tortillas
Halal	✔	Non-Halal meat like Pork and ducks	
Kosher	✔	Non-Kosher Meat like pork and ducks Non-Kosher cheese	Kosher meat like lamb, beef and chicken Vegetables Vegetarian cheese
Paleo diet	✔	Tortillas with wheat, Barley, rice, corn and rye	Paleo tortillas made from coconut flour, almond flour or sesame seeds flour
Macrobiotic diet	✔	Meat from animals Cheese from animals, Tortillas with refined white flour, and white rice flour	Vegetables, Vegetarian cheese Paleo tortillas made from coconut flour, almond flour or sesame seeds flour
Fitness Program diet	✔	Tortillas with refined white flour, and white rice flour	Vegetables, Paleo tortillas made from coconut flour, almond flour or sesame seeds flour
Diabetic	✔	Tortillas with refined white flour, and white rice flour	Paleo tortillas made from coconut flour, almond flour or sesame seeds flour
Celiac disease	✔	Tortillas with wheat, Barley and rye	Corn tortillas Paleo Tortillas
Vegetarian	✔	Meat from animals Cheese from animals	Corn tortillas Paleo Tortillas Vegetarian cheese
Children	✔		

Mexican Wrapped Taco

Preparation time: 7 minutes

Leftover foods: Cooked meat, cooked vegetables

Ingredients:

1 cup cooked meat cut into small strips (Optional and substitutable)

1 cup cooked vegetables cut into small strips (Optional and substitutable)

½ sachet taco powder dissolved into ¼ cup water
4 Tortillas White whole wheat or whole wheat (Substitutable)

Garnishes:

1 medium onion cut into Julienne strips
1 medium tomato cut into Julienne strips, seeds removed
2 cups shredded cabbage or lettuce (optional)
1 fresh avocado sliced or chopped
½ cup taco sauce
½ cup Guacamole (optional)
½ cup Grated cheese (optional)

1. **Heat medium saucepan on medium heat. Add cooked meats or cooked vegetables and then sauté for 3 minutes. Add the taco powder mixture then stir until dried.**

2. **Remove from the saucepan and put in bowl and serve with garnishes.**

3. **Serve the tortillas but leave in the package so they don't dry easily.**

You are	Who can eat?	You can't eat (Optional)	Substitution
Gluten free non-celiac Sensitivity	✔	Tortillas with wheat, Barley and rye	Corn tortillas Paleo Tortillas made from coconut flour, almond flour or sesame seeds flour Vegetables and fruits
Halal	✔		
Kosher	✔	Non-Kosher Cheese	Vegetable, Kosher cheese Vegetarian cheese Fruits
Paleo diet	✔	Tortillas with wheat, Barley, rice, corn and rye	Paleo tortillas made from coconut flour, almond flour or sesame seeds flour
Macrobiotic diet	✔	Cheese made from animals, Tortillas with refined white flour, and white rice flour	Vegetables Vegetarian cheese Fruits
Fitness Program diet	✔	Tortillas with refined white flour, and white rice flour	Vegetables, Paleo tortillas Paleo tortillas
Diabetic	✔	Tortillas with refined white flour, and white rice flour	Paleo tortillas, Gluten free tortillas, whole wheat flour
Celiac disease	✔	Tortillas with wheat, Barley and rye	Corn tortillas Paleo Tortillas Fruits
Vegetarianism	✔	Cheese made from animals	Corn tortillas Paleo Tortillas Vegetarian cheese
Children	✔		

Fruit Cocktail Quesadillas

Fruit Cocktail Quesadillas

Preparation time: 6 minutes

Leftover foods: Fruit cocktail, tortillas

Ingredients:

¼ cup salsa (medium)
1 ½ cups grated cheddar cheese (Optional and substitutable)

3 tablespoons kidney beans (Optional)

3 tablespoons canned crush pineapple

3 tablespoons canned fruit cocktail

3 tablespoons canned corn

1 Package small size corn tortillas or white whole wheat cut in half (substitutable)

¼ cup Parmesan cheese (optional)

1. **Heat nonstick skillet or medium size frying pan over moderate heat. Add the grated cheese and salsa then toss for 1 minute.**
2. **Add fruit cocktail, kidney beans, pineapple and corn kernels. Blend all ingredients for 2 minutes or until the cheese is melted and then pour onto corn tortillas and cover with the other half of the tortilla.**
3. **Fry the filled tortillas and cook 1 minute on each side.**
4. **Remove and sprinkle with Parmesan cheese.**
5. **Serve immediately**

You are	Who can eat?	You can't eat (Optional)	Substitution
Gluten free non-celiac Sensitivity	✔	Wheat, barley, rye bread	Tapioca flour, Gluten free bread, Leftover cooked vegetables
Halal	✔		
Kosher	✔	Non-Kosher Cheese	Vegetarian cheese, Kosher cheese
Paleo diet	✔	Cornstarch, Bread with wheat, Barley, rice, corn and rye	Paleo bread made from coconut flour, almond flour or sesame seeds flour
Macrobiotic diet	✔	Cheese made from animals, Bread made from refined white flour and rice flour	Vegetarian cheese, Paleo bread made from coconut flour, almond flour, whole-wheat flour or white whole-wheat flour.
Fitness Program diet	✔	Bread made from refined white flour and rice flour	Vegetarian cheese, Paleo bread made from coconut flour, almond flour, whole-wheat flour or white whole-wheat flour.
Diabetic	✔	Bread made from refined white flour and rice flour	Paleo bread made from coconut flour, almond flour, whole-wheat flour or white whole-wheat flour.
Celiac disease	✔	Cornstarch, Bread with wheat, Barley, rice, corn and rye	Tapioca flour, Gluten free bread, Cassava rice
Vegetarian	✔	Cheese made from animals	Vegetarian cheese, cassava rice
Children	✔		

Cheese Fondue with Leftover Bread

Preparation time: 8 minutes

Leftover foods: Bread

Ingredients:

1 cup dries white wine

1-tablespoon cornstarch

450 grams / 16 oz total of 1/3 each Gruyere cheese, Emmentaler and Appenzeller – grated (Substitutable)

1 tablespoon Kirsch (Brandy distilled from the fermented juice of cherries)

Pinch of nutmeg (optional)

1-cup gherkins

2 cup bread White whole wheat or whole wheat cut into medium dice (substitutable)

1. Blend cheese and cornstarch to a separate bowl.
2. Pour the wine into the saucepan and bring to simmer over moderate heat. Gradually add half of the cheese blended with cornstarch, save the other half for later.
3. Stir until the cheese melts, add the second half of the cheese and continue stirring until the cheese melts. When completely melted, pour the kirsch and nutmeg and stir well.
4. Transfer to a fondue pot and keep it low heat. Serve immediately with bread cubes and gherkins.

You are	Who can eat?	You can't eat (Optional)	Substitution
Gluten free non-celiac Sensitivity	✔	Stock or bouillon cubes with wheat, barley and rye	Gluten free stocks or bouillon cubes
Halal	✔		Halal stocks or vegetable stocks
Kosher	✔		Kosher stock, Vegetable stock
Paleo diet	✔	Kidney beans, Pasta from refined white flour, barley, rye, rice and corn	Paleo Macaroni pasta, paleo or gluten free stocks, Vegetable stocks
Macrobiotic diet	✔	Meat stock from animals, Pasta from refined white flour	Vegetable stock, Paleo Macaroni pasta, paleo or gluten free stocks, Vegetable stocks
Fitness Program diet	✔	Pasta from refined white flour	Vegetable stock, Paleo Macaroni pasta, paleo or gluten free stocks, Vegetable stocks
Diabetic	✔	Pasta from refined white flour	Paleo Macaroni pasta, paleo or gluten free stocks, Vegetable stocks
Celiac disease	✔	Stock or bouillon cubes with wheat, barley and rye	Gluten free stock or bouillon cubes
Vegetarian	✔	Meat stock from animals	Vegetable stock
Children	✔		

Vegetable Soup with Macaroni

Vegetable Soup with Macaroni

Preparation time: 12 minutes

Leftover Foods: Cooked Vegetable or Cooked macaroni pasta and vegetable stock, meat stock

Ingredients:

1 medium cooked carrot cubed or diced (From your leftover foods)

1 medium cooked zucchini cubed or diced (From your leftover foods)

1 medium onion red or green chopped

1-tablespoon olive oil

4 cups cooked chicken, other meat or vegetable stock (substitutable)

½ cup cooked macaroni (optional)

3 tablespoons tomato paste

1 small can kidney beans (optional)

1. Heat the oil in a medium saucepan. Sauté the first three vegetable ingredients then cover and cook about 6 minutes (If the vegetables are already cooked warm them for 3 minutes).

2. Add the stock, macaroni, tomato paste and the kidney beans. Bring to boil and simmer for 5 minutes or until the vegetables and macaroni are soft or tender.

3. Serve hot.

You are	Who can eat?	You can't eat (Optional)	Substitution
Gluten free non-celiac Sensitivity	✔	Tortillas with wheat, Barley and rye	Corn tortillas Paleo Tortillas
Halal	✔	Non-Halal meat like pork and ducks	Halal meat like lamb, beef and chickens
Kosher	✔	Non-kosher meat like Pork and ducks Cheese	Vegetarian Cheese Vegetables Kosher meat like lamb, beef and chickens
Paleo diet	✔	Tortillas with wheat, Barley, rice, corn and rye	Paleo tortillas made from coconut flour, sesame seeds flour, almond flour and flaxmeal seeds flour
Macrobiotic diet	✔	Meat from animals Cheese from animals, tortillas from refined processed white flour	Vegetarian cheese Whole wheat grain tortillas, paleo tortillas made from coconut flour
Fitness Program diet	✔	Tortillas from refined processed white flour	Vegetables, Whole wheat grain tortillas, paleo tortillas made from coconut flour
Diabetic	✔	Tortillas from refined processed white flour	Paleo tortillas made from coconut flour, almond flour or sesame seeds flour, Whole wheat grains
Celiac disease	✔	Tortillas with wheat, Barley and rye	Corn tortillas Paleo Tortillas
Vegetarianism	✔	Meat from animals Cheese from animals	Vegetables Vegetarian cheese
Children	✔		

Wrapped Leftover Foods

Preparation time: 12 minutes

Leftover foods: Cooked meats, cooked vegetables, salad dressing

Ingredients:

4 flour tortillas white whole wheat (substitutable)

¼ cup taco sauce mixed with 2 tablespoons fresh lemon juice

½ cup salad dressing (substitutable)

1-cup meat (optional and substitutable)

1-cup vegetables (optional and substitutable)

1 cup grated Cheddar cheese (optional)

Wax paper for baking cut the same size as the baking sheet

1. **Preheat oven to 375°F.**
2. **Arrange the meat and vegetables inside the tortillas then add the salad dressing.**
3. **Wrap the tortillas together with the fillings.**
4. **When everything is wrapped place on baking sheet then brush with tops with the taco sauce/lemon juice.**
5. **Spread the cheese on the top of the tortillas and bake for 8 minutes until the cheese melts and turns golden brown.**

6. Remove from the pan and wax paper and let it cool on a plate then serve.

    You can take this to the office easily.

You are	Who can eat?	You can't eat (Optional)	Substitution
Gluten free non-celiac Sensitivity	✔		
Halal	✔		
Kosher	✔	Non-Kosher Cheese, Fish no fins ans scales	Vegetarian cheese Kosher Cheese, Fish with fins and scales
Paleo diet	✔		
Macrobiotic diet	✔	Cheese from animals	Vegetarian cheese
Fitness Program diet	✔		
Diabetic	✔		
Celiac disease	✔		
Vegetarian	✔	Cheese from animals	Vegetarian cheese
Children	✔		

Baked Salmon

Baked Salmon

Preparation time: 12 minutes

Leftover foods: Cooked salmon

Ingredients:

½ slice cooked salmon fillet

2 tablespoons honey
½ cup fresh squeezed grapefruit juice or fresh squeezed orange juice

1 medium onion

1 medium ripe tomato

1 cup grated cheddar cheese (optional and substitutable)

2 tablespoons olive oil

4 rectangle cut butter or softened butter 2 tablespoons

1 cup sliced tomatoes cut into Julienne strips

1. **Preheat oven to 375°F.**
2. **Place fish in a loaf pan or Pyrex dish. Add onion first then fish, followed by tomatoes on top of the fish then pour the juice and honey over the fish.**
3. **Sprinkle grated cheese on top. Bake for 10-12 minutes or until the cheese is melted and turns to a golden brown.**
4. **Serve when it cools down.**

You are;	Who can eat?	You can't eat (Optional)	Substitution
Gluten free non-celiac Sensitivity	✔	Bread with wheat, Barley and rye Bouillon cubes or stock with wheat, Barley and rye	Gluten free Bread Gluten free bouillon cubes or stock Paleo bread
Halal	✔		
Kosher	✔	Non-kosher Cheese	Vegetarian cheese, kosher cheese
Paleo diet	✔	Bread with wheat, Barley, rice, corn and rye Bouillon cubes or stock with wheat, Barley and rye	Paleo bread made from coconut flour, flaxseed meal, cassava rice, almond flour and sesame seeds flour
Macrobiotic diet	✔	Cheese from animals	Vegetarian cheese
Fitness Program diet	✔	Bread with refined processed white flour	Paleo bread made from coconut flour, flaxseed meal, cassava rice, almond flour and sesame seeds flour
Diabetic	✔	Bread with refined processed white flour	Paleo bread made from coconut flour, flaxseed meal, cassava rice, almond flour and sesame seeds flour
Celiac disease	✔	Bread with wheat, Barley and rye Bouillon cubes or stock with wheat, Barley and rye	Gluten free Bread Gluten free bouillon cubes or stock Paleo bread
Vegetarian	✔	Cheese from animals	Vegetarian cheese
Children	✔		

French Onion Soup

French Onion Soup

Preparation time: 12 minutes

Leftover foods: Onions

Ingredients:

1 medium onion peeled and cut in medium strips

1 medium cans mushrooms (optional and substitutable)

1 baguette cut in squares (substitutable)

1 cup grated cheese (substitutable)

1½ cups beef or vegetable broth

1. Use a blender to blend the onions, broth and mushrooms until all solids are chopped. Then bring to boil on medium heat and simmer for 15 minutes.
2. Remove from the saucepan and pour into mugs and then put cheese on top. Cover with mug lid or aluminum foil for 2 minutes.
3. Serve when the cheese is all melted and put the bread on top.

PAN DE SAL BREADS

You are	Who can eat?	You can't eat (Optional)	Substitution
Gluten free non-celiac Sensitivity	✔	Bread with wheat, barley and rye	Gluten free bread dough
Halal	✔	Non-Halal meat like Pork and ducks	Halal meat like Lamb, beef, chicken Vegetables
Kosher	✔	Non-Kosher Meat like pork and ducks	Vegetables Kosher meat like lamb, beef, and chickens
Paleo diet	✔	Bread with wheat, barley, rice, corn and rye	Paleo bread dough from coconut flour, almond flour, sesame seeds flour, cassava rice, sweet potato rice and flaxseeds meal
Macrobiotic diet	✔	Meat form animals, Bread with, rice, Bread with refined processed white flour	Vegetables, Paleo bread dough from coconut flour, almond flour, sesame seeds flour, cassava rice, sweet potato rice and flaxseeds meal, Whole grains flour
Fitness Program diet	✔	Bread with wheat, barley, rice, corn and rye	Paleo dough
Diabetic	✔	Bread with wheat, barley, rice, corn and rye	Vegetables, Paleo bread dough from coconut flour, almond flour, sesame seeds flour, cassava rice, sweet potato rice and flaxseeds meal, Whole grains flour
Celiac disease	✔	Bread with wheat, barley and rye	Paleo Bread dough Gluten free bread dough
Vegetarian	✔	Meat from animals	Vegetables
Children	✔		

Pan de sal de Mexico Fajitas

Pan de sal de Mexico Fajitas

Preparation/Cooking time: 3 hours

Leftover foods: Cooked meats, fajitas mixtures, Cooked Vegetable

Ingredients:

Pandesal dough recipe on page 38 or Cassava rice dough (See page 40)

Filling:

2 cups Fajita mixture leftover food
2 cups cooked meat cut in julienne strips (Substitutable)
2 cups cooked vegetables julienned (Substitutable)
1 cup cooked bell pepper julienned
½ sachet Fajita powder dissolved in ½ cup water
1-cup taco sauce

1. Preheat oven to 375°F 15 minutes before the dough finishes rising.

2. Cook all filling ingredients together in a frying pan over medium heat for 4-5 minutes or until they become mostly dry.

3. See page 93 Mexican fajitas recipe for directions. Add 1-tablespoon taco sauce to the filling.

4. Bake for 8 minutes or until golden brown. Serve hot.

You are	Who can eat?	You can't eat (Optional)	Substitution
Gluten free non-celiac Sensitivity	✔	Bread with wheat, barley and rye	Gluten free bread dough, Paleo bread dough
Halal	✔	Non-Halal meat like Pork and ducks	Halal meat like Lamb, beef, chickens Vegetables
Kosher	✔	Non-Kosher Meat like Pork and ducks	Vegetables, Kosher meat like lamb, beef and chickens
Paleo diet	✔	Bread with wheat, barley, rice, corn and rye	Paleo bread dough from coconut flour, almond flour, sesame seeds flour, cassava rice, sweet potato rice and flaxseeds meal,
Macrobiotic diet	✔	Meat from animals, Bread with refined processed white flour, rice flour	Vegetables, Paleo bread dough from coconut flour, almond flour, sesame seeds flour, cassava rice, sweet potato rice and flaxseeds meal, Whole grains flour
Fitness Program diet	✔	Bread with refined processed white flour	Paleo bread dough
Diabetic	✔	Bread with refined processed white flour	Paleo bread dough from coconut flour, almond flour, sesame seeds flour, cassava rice, sweet potato rice and flaxseeds meal, Whole grains flour
Celiac disease	✔	Bread with wheat, barley and rye	Paleo Bread dough Gluten free bread dough
Vegetarian	✔	Meat from animals	Vegetables
Children	✔		

Pan de sal de Pilipinas Adobo

Pan de sal de Pilipinas Adobo

Preparation/Cooking time: 3 hours

Leftover foods: Cooked adobo, cooked meat, cooked vegetable

Ingredients:

Pan de sal recipe on page 38 or Cassava rice dough on page 40

Filling:

2 cups cooked meat adobo recipe or
2 cups cooked vegetable adobo on page 71

1. **Add filling inside the Pan de sal dough, put 1 tablespoon in each.**

You are	Who can eat?	You can't eat (Optional)	Substitution
Gluten free non-celiac Sensitivity	✔	Bread with wheat, barley and rye	Gluten free bread dough, Paleo bread dough
Halal	✔		
Kosher	✔	Non-Kosher Cheese	Vegetarian cheese, Kosher cheese
Paleo diet	✔	Bread with wheat, barley, rice, corn and rye	Paleo bread dough from coconut flour, almond flour, sesame seeds flour, cassava rice, sweet potato rice and flaxseeds meal
Macrobiotic diet	✔	Cheese from animals, Bread with refined processed white flour, rice flour	Paleo bread dough from coconut flour, almond flour, sesame seeds flour, cassava rice, sweet potato rice and flaxseeds meal, Whole grains flour Vegetarian cheese
Fitness Program diet	✔	Bread with refined processed white flour	Paleo bread dough from coconut flour, almond flour, sesame seeds flour, cassava rice, sweet potato rice and flaxseeds meal, Whole grains flour
Diabetic	✔	Bread with refined processed white flour	Paleo bread dough from coconut flour, almond flour, sesame seeds flour, cassava rice, sweet potato rice and flaxseeds meal, Whole grains flour
Celiac disease	✔	Bread with wheat, barley and rye	Paleo Bread dough from coconut flour, almond flour, sesame seeds flour, cassava rice, sweet potato rice and flaxseeds meal Gluten free bread dough
Vegetarian	✔	Cheese from animals	Vegetarian cheese
Children	✔		

Pan de sal de Queso (Cheese Bread)

Pan de sal de Queso (Cheese Bread)

Preparation/Cooking time: 3 hours

Leftover foods: Cheese

Ingredients:

Pan de sal recipe on page 38 or Cassava rice dough (page 40)

Filling:

2 cups diced cheese

1. **Preheat oven 375°F 15 minutes before the dough finishes rising.**
2. **Place the cheese inside the dough and seal.**

You are	Who can eat?	You can't eat (Optional)	Substitution
Gluten free non-celiac Sensitivity	✔	Bread with wheat, barley and rye	Gluten free bread dough
Halal	✔	Non-Halal meat like Pork and ducks	Halal meat like Lamb, beef, chickens Vegetables
Kosher	✔	Non-Kosher Meat like Pork and ducks	Vegetables, Kosher meat like lamb, beef and chickens
Paleo diet	✔	Bread with wheat, barley, rice, corn and rye	Paleo bread dough from coconut flour, almond flour, sesame seeds flour, cassava rice, sweet potato rice and flaxseeds meal
Macrobiotic diet	✔	Meat from animals, Bread with refined processed white flour, rice flour	Vegetables, Whole grains bread dough, Paleo bread dough from coconut flour, almond flour, sesame seeds flour, cassava rice, sweet potato rice and flaxseeds meal
Fitness Program diet	✔	Bread with refined processed white flour	Vegetables, Whole grains bread dough, Paleo bread dough from coconut flour, almond flour, sesame seeds flour, cassava rice, sweet potato rice and flaxseeds meal
Diabetic	✔	Bread with refined processed white flour	Vegetables, Whole grains bread dough, Paleo bread dough from coconut flour, almond flour, sesame seeds flour, cassava rice, sweet potato rice and flaxseeds meal
Celiac disease	✔	Bread with wheat, barley and rye	Paleo Bread dough Gluten free bread dough
Vegetarian	✔	Meat from animals	Vegetables
Children	✔		

Pan de sal Bavaria Germany

Pan de sal Bavaria Germany

Preparation/Cooking time: 3 hours

Leftover foods: Cooked sausages, cooked vegetable sausages

Ingredients:

Pan de sal dough recipe on page 38 or
Cassava rice dough (see on page 40)

Filling:

2 cups cooked meat sausages (optional and substitutable)

2 cups cooked vegetable sausages (optional and substitutable)

1-cup gravy

1. **Preheat oven to 375°F 15 minutes before the dough finishes rising.**
2. **Place the sausages inside the dough and seal. Cook using instructions on page 38 or 40.**

You are	Who can eat?	You can't eat (Optional)	Substitution
Gluten free non-celiac Sensitivity	✔	Bread with wheat, barley and rye	Gluten free bread dough, Plaeo bread dough
Halal	✔		
Kosher	✔		
Paleo diet	✔	Bread with wheat, barley, rice, corn and rye	Paleo bread dough from coconut flour, almond flour, sesame seeds flour, cassava rice, sweet potato rice and flaxseeds meal
Macrobiotic diet	✔	Bread with refined processed white flour	Paleo bread dough from coconut flour, almond flour, sesame seeds flour, cassava rice, sweet potato rice and flaxseeds meal, Whole grain bread dough
Fitness Program diet	✔	Bread with refined processed white flour	Paleo bread dough from coconut flour, almond flour, sesame seeds flour, cassava rice, sweet potato rice and flaxseeds meal
Diabetic	✔	Bread with refined processed white flour	Paleo bread dough from coconut flour, almond flour, sesame seeds flour, cassava rice, sweet potato rice and flaxseeds meal, Whole grain bread dough
Celiac disease	✔	Bread with wheat, barley and rye	Paleo Bread dough Gluten free bread dough
Vegetarian	✔		
Children	✔		

Pan de sal de Vegetarian

Pan de sal de Vegetarian

Preparation/Cooking time: 3 hours

Leftover foods: Cooked vegetables

Ingredients:

Pan de sal dough recipe on page 38 or
Cassava rice dough (page 40)

Filling:

2 cups cooked vegetables (optional and substitutable)
½ cup gravy or ½ cup cheese

1. Preheat oven 375°F 15 minutes the dough finishes rising.
2. Place the vegetables inside the dough and seal. Pan de sal instruction page 38 or 40.

Dummies Kitchen Diaries

Questions

What have you learned from Leftover Foods: Optional and Substitutable Ingredients?

How has it changed your reality and logical ideas concerning food?

Have you tried to create your own recipes from your "leftover foods"?

What is the name of your creative creation?

Please share your recipe and photo for the creative recipe you made. Please write in the next blank page.

Comments about the ideas in this book:

First Creative Creation From My "Leftover Foods"

_____
(Recipe name and Photo)

Preparation Time:

Leftover foods:

Ingredients:

Directions:

Please scan and send these two pages of DUMMIES KITCHEN DIARIES
To our online website.

My Personal Dummies checklist

My Name is:

_____

_____

Age: ____ Male: ____
Female: ____

Practice/Beliefs	I am ✔	I want to be ✔
Halal		
Kosher		
Gluten free Non-celiac sensitivity diet		
Fitness program diet		
Paleo diet		
Gluten free with celiac sensitivity diet		
Macrobiotic diet		
Ovo vegetarianism		
Lacto vegetarianism		
Ovo-lacto or lacto-ovo vegetarianism		
Jain vegetarianism		
Veganism		
Raw veganism		
Fruitarianism		
Buddhist vegetarianism		
Judaism vegetarianism		
Other way of diet (Specify Please)		

Question:
Are you willing to try to be _____?
Or are you _____?
Why?
Answer:

CPSIA information can be obtained
at www.ICGtesting.com
Printed in the USA
LVOW06s0505010416
R10756300001B/R107563PG481325LVX2B/1/P